Cracking Drama

Progression in Drama within English (5–16)

Paul Bunyan, John Catron, Larraine Harrison, Sean McEvoy,
Ruth Moore, Bill Welburn, Jane Williams

NATE

The contributors to this publication represent a wide spectrum of drama practice. The experience of a long-standing drama committee within an English association is unique. Expertise is derived from extensive classroom experience across all phases, advisory work, inspection and curriculum management.

Cracking Drama is published by the National Association for the Teaching of English (NATE), the UK subject teacher association for all aspects of the teaching of English from pre-school to university.

NATE
50 Broadfield Road
Sheffield S8 0XJ
Tel: 0114 255 5419
Fax: 0114 255 5296

British Library Cataloguing in Publication data. A catalogue record for this book is available from the British Library.

ISBN 0 901291 81 1

Printed in the United Kingdom by:
York Publishing Services Ltd
64 Hallfield Road
Layerthorpe
York YO31 7ZQ

Contents

Acknowledgements

The authors would like to thank the teachers and young people in the schools where the units appearing in this book have been trialled. Special thanks to the Royal Holloway College, where the initial planning meeting for this publication took place.

We are grateful to the following for permission to reproduce text and illustrations:

Text extracts (pages 56–8) and illustrations (pages 61–2) from *Five Secrets in a Box* by Catherine Brighton. Copyright © Catherine Brighton 1987. Reproduced by permission of the author c/o Rogers, Coleridge & White Ltd., 20 Powis Mews, London W11 1JN.

The poem 'Daniel' (page 76) reproduced by permission of the author Laura Forgette Crist.

Extracts (page 88) from *Bretevski Street* by Lin Coghlan reproduced by permission of PFD on behalf of Lin Coghlan.

We are grateful to the following for permission to reproduce photographs and illustrations:

John Williams, illustrations (pages 15, 20, 29, 32, 37, 41, 46, 54, 68, 90, 99); map of Padua (page 67), reproduced by permission of the Syndics of Cambridge University Library; photograph of children taken from Eastern Europe during the SS 'Heuaktion' (Hay Action), and temporarily imprisoned in Auschwitz awaiting their transfer to Germany (pages 73, 82), Instytut Pamieci Narodwej/Institute of National Memory, courtesy of USHMM Photo Archives; reproduction of 1597.15 3 title page *The Apprehension and confession of three notorious witches ... condemned and executed at Chelmsford* (page 88), reproduced by permission of Lambeth Palace Library.

Introduction

Drama in the National Curriculum

From the year 2000, the reviewed National Curriculum Orders for English has been put into practice in every school. Never before has drama had the status that it is given in this document. While drama continues to be a thriving and effective subject in its own right in a great many secondary schools, its strengthened position within English and its strong relationship with language development is made clear by this change. In all key stages, a specific strand of the curriculum refers to the making, performing and critical analysis of drama, demonstrating progression throughout.

Who is this book for?

Whether you are a drama specialist working in the context of the arts, or a teacher of English in the secondary school, whether you are a teacher or language co-ordinator with some experience of using drama techniques in the primary classroom, or if you have anxieties about the implications of these changes, this book has been designed to help you.

Progression

It has been understood, through research and practice, that children's experience of drama develops through structured play in the early years to young people's complex and selective use of drama techniques later in their lives. However, an understanding of the way progression takes place through drama within the English curriculum deserves to be more fully explored. This publication both defines that progression, particularly in relation to English and Literacy, and demonstrates, through tried and tested classroom practice, how it can be achieved.

Key Stages 1–4

To understand progression, teachers need to have a clear understanding of how pupils learn throughout all the key stages. For this reason, we have not attempted to divide this publication into primary and secondary sections. Good practice in primary drama teaching will be informed by a clear understanding of the higher-level skills achieved in the advanced stages of progression, while good secondary drama teaching will be informed by a clearer understanding of the way pupils have progressed through drama in the earlier stages.

Although this document can be used for curriculum ideas and in the development of schemes of work, we would encourage teachers, whatever their key stage specialism, to read and use this publication as a whole. It is designed to support teachers in developing their understanding of the progression process.

Knowing that all pupils progress in different ways and at different levels, teachers may find that many of the units can be used across all key stages.

The contributors

The contributors to this publication represent a wide spectrum of drama practice. The experience of a long-standing drama committee within an English association is unique. Its expertise is derived from extensive classroom experience across all phases, advisory work, inspection and curriculum management. The committee's work, not only with the National Association for the Teaching of English (NATE), but with National Drama and the International Drama Education Association (IDEA), enables the committee to offer regional, national and international perspectives, and has led them to examine in more detail the relationship between drama and English and the progression that can be achieved when this relationship is most effective.

The voices of individual members of the committee are represented throughout this book, together with a variety of approaches, styles and working contexts. Strength lies in these differences. Much debate and shared practice has converged, bringing a clearer understanding of the way in which progression in drama (in relation to English) occurs.

How to use this book

Section 1 explores the relationship between drama and English, and explains in more detail the background to this publication.

Following this, in Section 2, is a detailed exploration of the nature of progression in drama within English. With the use of diagrams and examples drawn from Section 3, it sets out the nature of this progression and the different skills that pupils demonstrate at different levels of their learning experience.

Section 3 provides a series of teaching units (arranged chronologically), which demonstrate how progression can be encouraged and achieved through good classroom practice.

The nature of drama

What is it to say that a pupil has made progress in drama? This book aims to answer that question with a clear theoretical statement, grounded and exemplified in the real teaching practice of the writers.

Progression in English

We know what to look for when we want to justify a claim that a pupil's learning has progressed in English. We are used to applying specific descriptors to a pupil's abilities, skills and knowledge in order to make that judgement. Certain levels of attainment are expected to be achieved by the majority of pupils in the National Curriculum. In drama there exist clear assessment criteria for judging pupils' achievement at GCSE and A level, but there is not yet a clear framework that sets out what progress in drama in English means across the years of compulsory education. This publication aims to do that.

Progression in drama within English

Progress in drama requires an extension and maturation in the pupil's ability to engage, analyse and transfer understanding. Learning will be social, communicative, artistic, aesthetic, imaginative and rational, and will develop an understanding both of the conventions and methods of the art form. Its subject matter in the English classroom will address emotional, social, personal and political issues. In this first chapter we illustrate this contention by explaining what we take drama to be.

What do pupils learn in drama?

The National Association for the Teaching of English, in its Position Paper on drama, published in 1998, defined the subject as 'the expression of meaning through the enactment of events'.

In the educational drama we are talking about (which is not the related process of training pupils to perform theatre), pupils create, re-create or enact events by means of drama conventions. These conventions are the techniques that are used to structure dramatic activity and are drawn from theatre, literature, the cinema and multimedia. When pupils and teachers do drama together, they apply these conventions to the material on which they are working. As they do so they are learning the aesthetic and creative skills involved in the choice and application of the conventions, but they are also learning to work with others and to express themselves in a variety of imaginary and therefore personally safe arenas. They are also learning directly from their active engagement with the content and subject matter of the lesson.

Drama conventions and progression

Examples of the drama conventions can be found in all of the units set out in this book, as well as in the Glossary at the end. Section 2 explains how the application of these conventions, by both pupils and teachers, can be a means of ensuring that pupils are progressing in their studies.

What is unique about drama?

What is unique about drama is the fact that all the pupils' enactive work takes place in a fictional environment, the boundaries of which are clearly defined. The clear boundary means that in acting as someone somewhere else, pupils look at their lives, identities, values and cultures in a place where their real status and identity is not at stake. Individual and communal self-esteem is strengthened through the drama as the individual sees the world from other perspectives. That boundary between the drama and real life must always be very clear. It must also be clear that, within the structures and conventions of the art form and the lesson, the pupils are free to take the drama wherever it seems right for them to go.

Engagement

Pupils doing drama are engaged as whole people, not merely as functions within an institution as they are within the confines of a role-play. For example, a pupil in a role-play about a local radio station putting together a news broadcast cannot decide to challenge a decision on an issue of principle, as they could in a drama lesson, much less go back into the journalist's life in his/her imagination to discover why they feel so strongly about the issue.

Effective learning

Discipline and integrity are watchwords in good drama. They are requirements for effective learning. Students learn to respect themselves, others and the art form, because they can see the value of the learning that is happening. They learn for themselves the value of work in which they have made an investment, compared to work that is merely mimicry or burlesque.

Reflection and analysis

A crucial element in any drama work, however, often takes place outside the drama – though it can very fruitfully take place within it, too. This is reflection and analysis, where pupils and teacher look back on the work and consider the particular meanings generated by their work and that of others. They consider the thoughts and feelings that have emerged in the work and recognise the new ideas that have arisen about the issues in the session – ideas perhaps about themselves and their lives and the lives of others. They will also, eventually, reflect on the content and the expression of that content.

The initial role of the teacher

The teacher will start by providing the initial stimulus, which may be a text familiar or unfamiliar to the pupils, or visual images, or documents, or perhaps the teacher working in role. Usually, some sort of narrative is developed, with the teacher intervening at different moments, both in and out of role – perhaps to introduce a problem for the pupils to solve. This may mean slowing down the action through the use of one or more conventions; or delving into the past or looking forward to the future in order to discover the causes and consequences of particular decisions and actions taking place now in the drama.

Presentation skills

All educational drama contains some element of performance, though this is not of course the end product to be assessed as if it were a piece of theatre. Nevertheless, pupils will acquire skills of presentation – of acting. Within the English curriculum they should learn how to communicate clearly and expressively. They will learn how to work together in a team to put across ideas and emotions to their colleagues and friends. Their collaborative achievements can be public, and submitted for the scrutiny of their peers.

Drama and English

Drama exists as an academic subject in its own right at GCSE and A level for those who choose to study it. It is also included in the English Curriculum Orders as part of young people's core entitlement. This is most effectively done in an integrated way.

Speaking and listening

Many English teachers acknowledge that drama provides a safe and exciting forum for developing the pupils' skills in speaking and listening in a wide range of contexts. Drama puts young people in situations, formal and informal, that they may never encounter in their lives outside the classroom, and requires the use of discourses and registers they would not otherwise use. In the drama, however, they are learning to use them because they need to in the role they have developed. They can see the point and purpose of using language in a way they wouldn't normally because it is an appropriate part of the fiction to which they belong. This happens because drama allows the pupils to engage actively, analyse critically and transfer their understanding to other areas of learning. Drama is an effective way to get young people to use, reflect on and understand the nature of spoken and heard language. The classroom is a place where young people must plan, negotiate, think on their feet and solve problems, as well as reflect upon their experience in their own words.

Reading

Drama work that takes literary, non-literary or media texts as its subject matter enables pupils to explore issues, characters, language and contexts in a way that engages them and takes them inside that text. It enables them to use their imagined experience and improvised language to illuminate the material being studied and learn about its ideas and the function of its language in a critical way. Pupils' experience of drama means that when they are working with playscripts they bring their performance knowledge to the page and come to a ready understanding of the theatrical conventions of the form and the ways that language on the page represents a blueprint for performance.

Writing

Because pupils are engaged in the drama, the fictional context offers many oportunities for different types of writing, for a variety of audiences and purposes: letters, diaries, reports, scripts, notices, persuasive writing, journalism, narratives and poems can all flow naturally out of the drama. When they write these tasks they usually do not feel it is just an exercise; often, it motivates them to want to become competent writers.

Drama, then, can be at the heart of pupils' learning in the English classroom for speaking and listening, reading and writing. But it can also be just as invaluable in humanities, social studies and personal education. There is no doubt, either, of its value in educating pupils in Citizenship.

Assessment and progression

Work emerging from drama work in the English classroom, whether spoken or written, can be assessed in its own right as a piece of English work. For this assessment to be formative, English teachers need to be able to recognise in their pupils:

- the ability to collaborate with others, in order to respond appropriately to the needs of the group

- understanding and knowledge of drama genres, concepts and conventions, and the skill to apply these ideas artistically to make meanings and represent life

- the ability to perform and communicate creatively, employing a range of skills

- the ability to reflect on and respond to the drama that has been created and to understand what has been learned from the experience

- the ability to evaluate critically their own drama work and that of others

- the knowledge and understanding of the subject matter or issues that have been the content of the lesson, where appropriate

- the ability to apply the above to other areas of the English curriculum.

Pupils can demonstrate their abilities through the use of discussion, logs, profiles, journals, imaginative writing, diagrams, art work and multimedia artefacts produced by the pupils themselves, as well as by the teacher recording her or his impressions of the work soon after it happens.

This, then, is the basis of assessment in drama. Precisely what we mean by progression in drama is explained in Section 2.

Progression through engagement, critical analysis and transference

Progression

The purpose of this book is to explain and exemplify how pupils can make progress in their learning by using drama approaches in English. Progression is defined here as *the evidenced development in learning which takes place when drama methodology is applied to teaching and learning in English.*

Throughout the rest of this section, examples from the units are drawn upon to illustrate progression.

Drama is in a unique position in the curriculum because it offers the opportunity for pupils to engage so completely in an imaginative world whilst simultaneously holding on to the objectivity and detachment of the real world. This dual position crucially allows pupils to perceive in different ways at the same time. The aims and outcome of the teaching and learning may vary but what remains central is the uniqueness created by this engagement. Subjective and objective understanding happen simultaneously, as do emotional involvement and critical thinking.

Examples

In Unit 10, the drama focuses on the life of the astronomer Galileo undertaken with children at Key Stage 2. The class might be working in pairs employing a 'guided tour' convention to explore the seventeenth-century city in the drama. One leading the other, they work from a projected map or picture to explore the historical or geographical environment depicted and simultaneously explore the space of the classroom and their collaborative relationship. (page 64)

In Unit 8, on 'The Emperor's new clothes', when the pupils are asked to demonstrate their ideas concerning royalty, the subjective experience of creating the 'Kingship' tableaux works hand-in-hand with the objective analysis needed to construct 'frames' that are authentic. (page 47)

The use of the e-mails from Kosovo in Unit 12, 'Drama and ICT,' allows pupils subjectively to explore the lives of the two young people while objectively questioning the differences between them as well as wider issues about war and reality. They are emotionally engaged in the drama while at the same time thinking critically about the medium of communication, the symbolic use of drama and the different meanings created (and the relevance of) the language used. (page 81)

It is this position, process and deliberate focus on the imaginative and the real, the creative and the analytical, that leads to pupils becoming more aware of drama's methods and more proficient in their application, leading to a development in their critical analysis skills and their capacity to transfer those critical processes to other texts/ideas. It is because pupils themselves are experiencing, and therefore learning, the skills of construction and deconstruction that progression in drama means that there is a real potential for progress in English.

Examples

In Unit 8, pupils are asked to share their tableaux and respond as onlookers to what they see as contributing to their reading of 'Kingship/royalty' from the visual text. Attempting interpretations in this way encourages vocabulary extension and descriptive language. (page 47)

In Unit 14, through their use of drama conventions to explore the links between the three stories, pupils develop high order skills of comparison through the recognition of authorial styles, imagery used, the structure of the texts and the specific language employed. The drama directly involves pupils in understanding how texts are constructed, helping to develop analytical skills that they can transfer to other situations in English. (page 91)

Central to this progression is the capacity of the teacher to intervene in the learning. Judicious teacher intervention in pupils' learning can occur:

- *within* the drama, to create a framework of dramatic understanding and progression

- *between* the imaginary world of drama and the real world of the pupil, to foster analysis, emotional engagement and critical thinking

- *beyond* the drama, to transfer the critical insights and learning processes to other symbolic texts.

Examples

So, later in Unit 10, when the guided tour is momentarily 'frozen', the teacher in role as a character from the drama intervenes to fill the silence with a short monologue introducing the character or perhaps narrates to move the drama on. (page 64)

In Unit 8, when pupils are involved as artisans designing items for the 'Royal Exhibition', the teacher can, as the 'Royal Chancellor,' refocus the pupils onto their essential loyalty to the King by a judicious repetition of the 'Oath of Allegiance'. This not only enhances their commitment to role but also allows the drama to move inevitably to a dénouement involving their willing complicity in deceiving the King. (page 50)

Also in Unit 8, when the pupils are first listening to the story it becomes necessary to stop in order to negotiate the 'drama contract' whereby pupils agree to 'pretend' in order to recreate the King's Coronation and Oath of Allegiance. (page 48)

In a third example from Unit 8, at the end, the pupils seek to redress the 'wrong' they have done to the King. This is the time when the teacher can extend the range of this new experience and understanding. It should not now be beyond the pupils' capabilities to grasp the 'tragic flaw' of King Lear, revealed in the first scene of the play by William Shakespeare. (page 52)

In Unit 15, on *Macbeth,* the work on transforming the details of the Sergeant's speech into statuary that has a dramatic impact requires close analytical reading of Shakespeare's language. (page 100)

At the end of the work on Unit 15, pupils will have been given an insight into the different political perspectives of the early modern and mediaeval periods, and will be able to reflect on the possibilities of making moral judgements about times and societies very different to our own.

Engagement

When pupils begin actively to engage in the imaginative world of drama, they are in the initial stages of a potentially dynamic continuum. Their early experiences may be characterised by simple play in an unstructured and informal context.

Example

One example would be building a puppet stage environment with toys or materials otherwise used in the play corner.

Participation in the drama at this level may be unselfconscious with only a tentative awareness of the imaginary world pupils are entering. They may be engaged in making sense of their experiences through a belief in their role and may also be emotionally engaged with the experience – but there will be fewer layers and limited depth to their engagement.

Examples

In Unit 3, dealing with caring for the environment, pupils initially take on roles as visitors to a beautiful place and enjoy miming the activities they have chosen to do there. This dramatic play contributes to their sense of ownership of the material and helps build belief in the drama. It is also the first step towards a deeper engagement, which helps motivate pupils to talk and write within and around the topic. (page 25)

In Unit 8, allowing the pupils to 'play' at royalty and status is a deliberate invitation to them to experiment with their own space, body and voice. Such a strategy so early in the theme is less about creating believable drama and much more about confidence-building, establishing teacher/pupil trust and enabling pupils to participate at their own level of competence. Such work lays the foundation for better chances of success as the drama work becomes more challenging. (page 47)

The teacher's role is to plan appropriate interventions into the process so that pupils gain an understanding of drama, how it works and how they can manipulate the art form for their own learning needs. Progression will then take place.

Examples

The teacher might introduce the role of a puppet with a problem to be solved, such as the concerns the puppet (who is just about to start school) might have about being able to make friends. The puppet, through the teacher, asks the children for their help.

In Unit 2, the teacher intervenes in the Humpty Dumpty freeze-frames to encourage very young children to view a moment in a story from the perspectives of the characters. The teacher's intervention also acts as an early model of textual analysis by implying that there could be different versions of the same moment, e.g. 'Should Humpty be smiling as he sits on the wall or should he look scared?' ... 'Did he think he was safe or did he think he was going to fall?' This suggests to young children that characters and events in stories and rhymes can be discussed as if they were real and that people can have different opinions. (page 21)

In Unit 8 the teacher's appropriate intervention is essential. Without such groundwork being laid the crucial 'revelation scene' cannot take place. But if the groundwork on role-play and pupil commitment to the drama has been done, there should be no problem changing roles and moving the drama forward.

As pupils' engagement with the role and the drama deepens, there is a growing implicit awareness of the medium and its power; their responses become more thoughtful and considered and their appreciation of the needs of the drama become more subtle and sophisticated. (See Figure 1.)

Figure 1: Engagement

The diagram below illustrates the progression that is taking place. The different strands identified within the ribbon of engagement will not all be developed at the same time. Thus, according to the student, the learning environment, the nature of the activity and perhaps most importantly the intervention of the teacher, the different aspects of progression will vary. Progression overall will be seen, however. Later we will see in diagrammatic form how this progression in engagement leads to progression in critical analysis and transference.

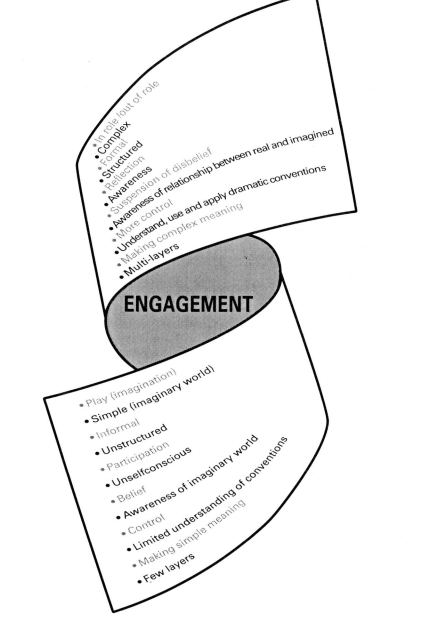

Examples

In Unit 9, when Virginia is told about the letter from the Vatican by her father, the pupils' responses to the dilemma Galileo and Virginia find themselves in are made manifest through the use of a *thought-tracking* or *conscience-alley* convention. (page 59)

In Unit 8, the pupils' willingness to become involved in a subterfuge will lead them to realise the implications of their 'acting in role'. They will show signs of guilt, regret and shame and may even attempt to extricate themselves from the situation. (page 52)

These initial stages of progression are reflected in the pupils' progression in English, where engagement with the role and their developed understanding mean that they begin to develop the skills of communication, analysis and reflection.

Examples

In Unit 9, the artisans are left with the consequences of their actions. It is then that they need to come out of role and, working with the teacher, think through and rationalise what can be done to put things right again. (page 52)

> In Unit 12, the use of 'role on the wall' for an exploration of the Bretevs and the Samacs requires pupils, after they have engaged with the roles, to think critically about the information that they are given and analyse the text in detail. (page 79)

The teacher is also able to intervene to extend pupils' awareness of the relationship between the real and imagined world and the way in which the selective use of drama conventions can develop this awareness.

Examples

In Unit 8, if the pupils do not respond to the 'Con Shark' visual stimulus, then 'freeze-frames' and 'coming out of role' and 'returning to the last moment of the drama' are strategies that will enable pupils to manipulate real and fictitious time in order to facilitate further development. (page 50)

Pupils are progressing in two parallel ways here; they are becoming more adept at working subjectively within the drama and, at the same time, they are objectively becoming aware of the complexities and possibilities of the medium. (See Figure 1.)

Examples

In Unit 8, the experience of a duplicity and its outcome can be used to encourage pupils to question the outcome of 'their actions' and, through pair, small group and whole class discussions, come to a better understanding of the human condition. Pupils will also have had the opportunity to refine their skills of stepping in and out of role. (page 52)

In Unit 15, pupils who play out Macbeth's dilemma about killing Duncan in both their own and Shakespeare's language become subjectively aware of the emotional and moral experience he is going through. They are also aware of the way both their own work and Shakespeare's language structures and produces emotions and ideas – both for themselves and their audience. (page 102)

Critical analysis

At this stage, pupils will move from a literal interpretation of ideas/texts, where their focus has been on the content and/or surface features, to a more detailed analysis of the symbolic, abstract or structure.

Example

In Unit 8, pupils are led towards the moral dilemma of condoned subterfuge. It is here that sensitive questioning and comments, as well as reactions from the teacher in role as the King, should elicit a growing understanding about the situation in which they are involved. (page 51)

Engaged participants in drama are driven to seek meaning because they are emotionally involved – and this affective response leads to cognitive understanding.

Examples

In Unit 8, by the end of the dramatic experience pupils will seek to atone for their active involvement in a duplicity against the King. The active engagement in the drama stimulates thinking processes that will lead them to understand the need to devise a way of resolving matters and making everyone feel better. (page 53)

In Unit 5, even pupils who briefly take on roles as Beowulf's fellow warriors during the Literacy Hour can become motivated to read extracts of the poem and strive to complete pieces of writing in a similar style. (page 34)

In Unit 6, the pupils in role as the farmers will seek to use and apply their knowledge of the story in order to explain their treatment of the Iron Man to a visitor. (page 38)

It is, therefore, the uniqueness of the relationship between the creative and the real, the subjective and the objective, the emotional and the cognitive which means that the skills of critical analysis are developed and drama becomes a powerful medium for developing progression in English. (See Figure 2.)

Examples

In Unit 12, through initial work on the book *Rose Blanche* by Roberto Innocenti, one of the images from the book is depicted through the use of slow-moving tableaux and masks. The scene, stimulated by an episode in the book, depicts the young German girl Rose passing food through a fence to the Jewish children in a concentration camp. The slow movement is interrupted by the teacher, who reads the poem 'Daniel' by Laura Forgette Crist, which deals with a mother's relationship with her little son in such a camp. The interruption of the poem, along with the work in role, encourages pupils to focus on the relationship between the writer, the reader and the text and to transfer this understanding to the wider subject, a current event or an aspect of their own lives. (page 76)

In Unit 8, the experience of a duplicity and the subsequent understanding of the need to 'put things right' provides numerous possibilities for extension work, including such things as written letters of apology, sympathy and/or advice, redrafting Oaths of Allegiance, designing the 'real' Royal Robes, and further drama work. Such work is excellent practice in writing and presenting for different audiences. (page 53)

Figure 2: Critical analysis

The diagram below illustrates the progression in critical analysis that is taking place. The different strands identified within the ribbon of critical analysis will not all be developed at the same rate and at the same time. Thus, according to the student, the learning environment, the nature of the activity and perhaps most importantly the level of engagement, the different aspects of progression will vary. Progression overall will be seen, however. English teachers might argue that this progression takes place away from the drama context. This is certainly true but it is the relationship that exists between engagement and critical analysis and transference that we believe is significant when looking at how progression takes place. Later we will see this inter-relationship in diagrammatic form.

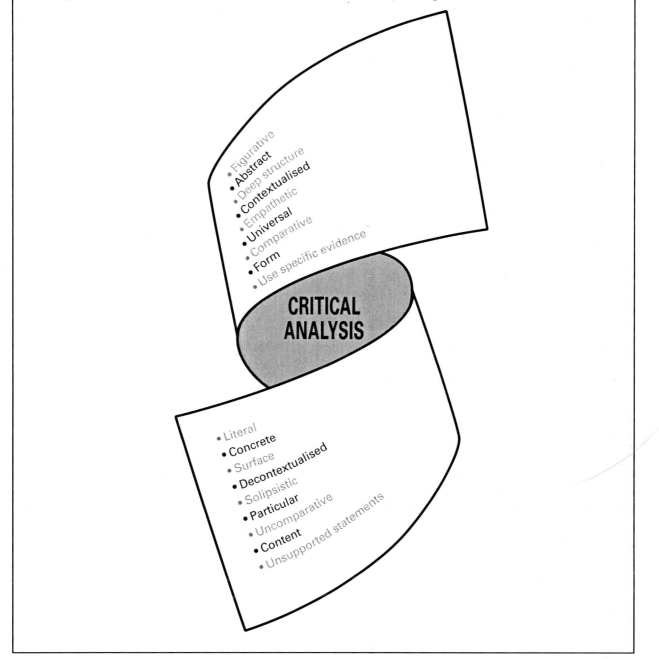

Drama demands critical thinking *and* emotional engagement on the part of participants. Regular and planned drama approaches that confront pupils with a need for critical analysis, creativity and deconstruction will move them from a superficial response to an awareness of, and developed skills in, critical thinking. (See Figure 2.)

Examples

In Unit 8, it is up to the teacher in role (as the King) to expose the pupils (in role as his loyal subjects) to such astute interrogation that they are then more able to recognise their culpability in the duplicitous affair, more able to suggest numerous ideas to redress the wrong done to the King and more keen to do further drama work so as to accomplish the need for healing. (page 53)

In Unit 15, pupils are asked to devise, within the 'safety' of the drama, a code of moral and civic values that will be contrasted with those of both Shakespeare's England and his depiction of feudal Scotland. Critical thinking and the skills of argument – logical and rhetorical presentation – are crucial here. (page 102)

Transference

The final stage of progression is the pupils' ability to transfer these skills to other texts/ ideas. It is the enactment that makes drama central to this progression. When pupils are emotionally engaged and analyse both in and out of role, they are actively developing the skills and understanding that are central to progression in English. Through this process, they recognise the layers that exist, analyse the methods and purposes employed, and gain an understanding of the intended audience and the use of different narrative structures. They are not, however, outside searching for clues to find a way in. They are deep within, experiencing for themselves the construction and layering of roles, issues, dilemmas and texts. They are also able to step outside to gain an additional important perspective. It is this ability to do both that indicates that their skills are so highly developed that, given a new situation, text or dilemma, the pupils are able to transfer their engagement and awareness of the drama, together with their analytical skills, to a new situation. Teacher intervention at this stage, therefore, is not as necessary. (See Figure 3.)

Examples

In Unit 14, therefore, the pupils are not developing analytical skills specific to the three stories but are developing high order reading skills that they will transfer to texts they have not seen before. This means that their formal GCSE assignments at the end of this unit will contain personal response and individual critical analysis rather than the teacher-led comments that sometimes derive from a more traditional approach to analysing text in the English classroom. (page 98)

In Unit 12, while focusing on specific aspects of the Holocaust and Kosovo, pupils are developing analytical skills through their engagement with the drama that will encourage them to explore authorial purpose, choice of communication, imagery and symbolism and the much wider issues of conflict in other as yet unknown situations. (page 73)

Drama is essentially issue-based, and confronting dilemmas of a moral, social or spiritual nature makes further demands on the participants' critical faculties. This will entail exploration of a wide variety of human relationships. By engaging in this collaborative process, however, pupils will learn to view the world from a variety of perspectives and come to an awareness of the universality of human experience. This sense of the personal and the universal is again central to the progression that is taking place. In drama both are experienced simultaneously and it is this understanding of the relationship of the two that is important to the learning process in English.

Examples

Drama, being as it is, a subject that asks profound questions, can sometimes even call into question notions such as 'the universal'. In Unit 15, for example, pupils are asked to experience, draw up, contrast and reflect on historically different attitudes to killing, the monarchy and authority in general. This requirement, in turn, invites pupils to reflect on what, if anything, might be 'universal' across different historical periods and raises the question of how, if at all, moral systems can be measured. (page 102)

In Unit 8, the pupils' participation in the development of the work within English will have involved them in exploring the possible moral and social implications of integrity. (page 52)

Figure 3: Transference

The diagram below illustrates the progression in transference that is taking place. The different strands identified within the ribbon of transference will not all be developed at the same rate and at the same time. Thus, according to the student, the learning environment, the nature of the activity and perhaps most importantly the level of engagement and critical analysis, the different aspects of progression will vary. Progression overall will be seen, however. English teachers might argue that this progression takes place away from the drama context. This is certainly true but it is the relationship that exists between engagement and critical analysis and transference that we believe is significant when looking at how progression takes place. Later we will see this inter-relationship in diagrammatic form.

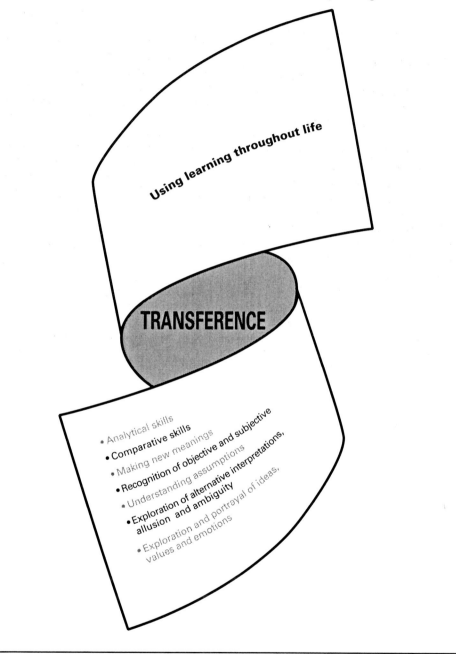

Two models of progression

The nature of progression, described above, should not be confined to a narrow definition or single exemplification. For this reason, the two models in Figure 4 are used to illustrate the effect that drama has on both the teaching and learning in English and the progression that takes place. It must be recognised that, depending on the pupil, the nature of the activity, the level of engagement and the intervention of the teacher, progression may occur in different ways.

Model 1: Complex ribbons of progression
The first model illustrates the complex nature of progression that leads to a truly linear description being inappropriate. The ribbons (illustrating the different strands of progression, engagement, critical analysis and transference) all move upwards demonstrating that progression is taking place. It is important to recognise, however, that none of them can exist without the others and that they may be happening simultaneously or certainly they may overlap and change places at times. Like ribbons round a maypole, the strands cross over and progression can take place at a different pace in some of the strands and not in others. What must be recognised is that progression can be recognised and identified within all three areas and that all three have a direct influence on each other, which creates the overall movement upwards.

Model 2: Sequential ribbons of progression
The second model separates the ribbons to form one long ribbon. This illustrates another form of progression that can be identified in the English classroom when drama is used. This diagram shows that, at times, a slightly more linear sense of progression can be understood, where, for example, high-order critical analysis skills, and therefore transference, are not possible without progression having taken place in engagement. At the initial stages of engagement, critical analysis is possible, but for contextualised, empathetic and comparative critical analysis to take place, engagement must have been developed as complex.

Taking the two diagrams together, it can be seen that, at different times, with different learners and with different teacher interventions, progression may take place in different ways. What is central to both models is the importance that engagement has on progression, and it is here that we begin to see the real impact that drama has on the English curriculum. It could be argued that critical analysis and transference can be developed in other activities within the English classroom. What these models and the units of work detailed in this book provide, however, is an insight into the way that drama effectively leads to progression in English. Engagement, and progression in engagement, are vital in this process.

Progression is complex. Within each ribbon there are many strands of progression that relate to teaching and learning. Teachers need to be able to recognise this and plan their interventions accordingly. What is simple, however, amidst this complexity, is the fundamental recognition of the effect that drama can have on both the learning process and the progression that takes place in English.

Figure 4: Model 1

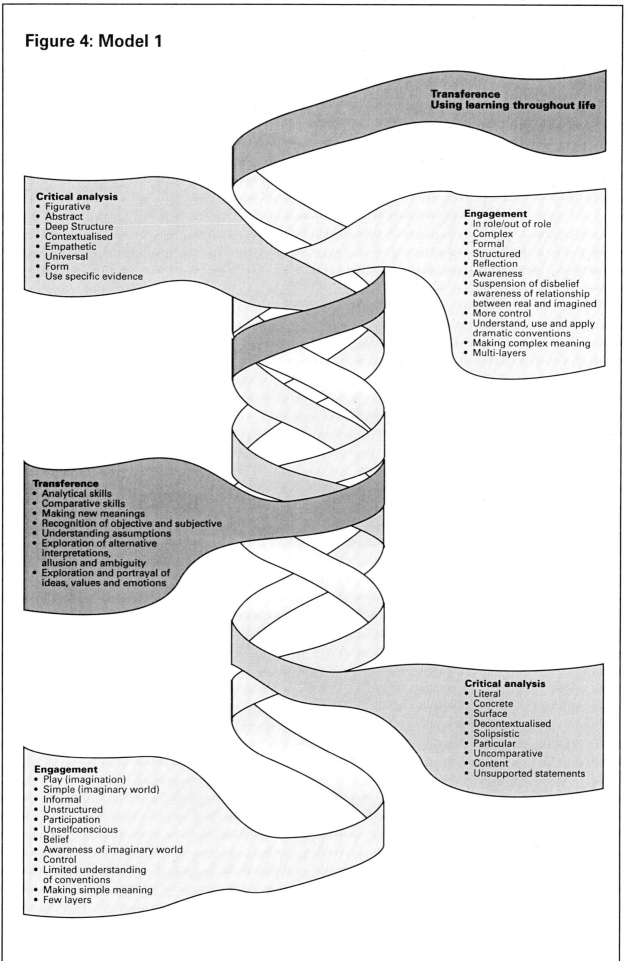

Transference
Using learning throughout life

Critical analysis
• Figurative
• Abstract
• Deep Structure
• Contextualised
• Empathetic
• Universal
• Form
• Use specific evidence

Engagement
• In role/out of role
• Complex
• Formal
• Structured
• Reflection
• Awareness
• Suspension of disbelief
• awareness of relationship
  between real and imagined
• More control
• Understand, use and apply
  dramatic conventions
• Making complex meaning
• Multi-layers

Transference
• Analytical skills
• Comparative skills
• Making new meanings
• Recognition of objective and subjective
• Understanding assumptions
• Exploration of alternative
  interpretations,
  allusion and ambiguity
• Exploration and portrayal of
  ideas, values and emotions

Critical analysis
• Literal
• Concrete
• Surface
• Decontextualised
• Solipsistic
• Particular
• Uncomparative
• Content
• Unsupported statements

Engagement
• Play (imagination)
• Simple (imaginary world)
• Informal
• Unstructured
• Participation
• Unselfconscious
• Belief
• Awareness of imaginary world
• Control
• Limited understanding
  of conventions
• Making simple meaning
• Few layers

Figure 4: Model 2

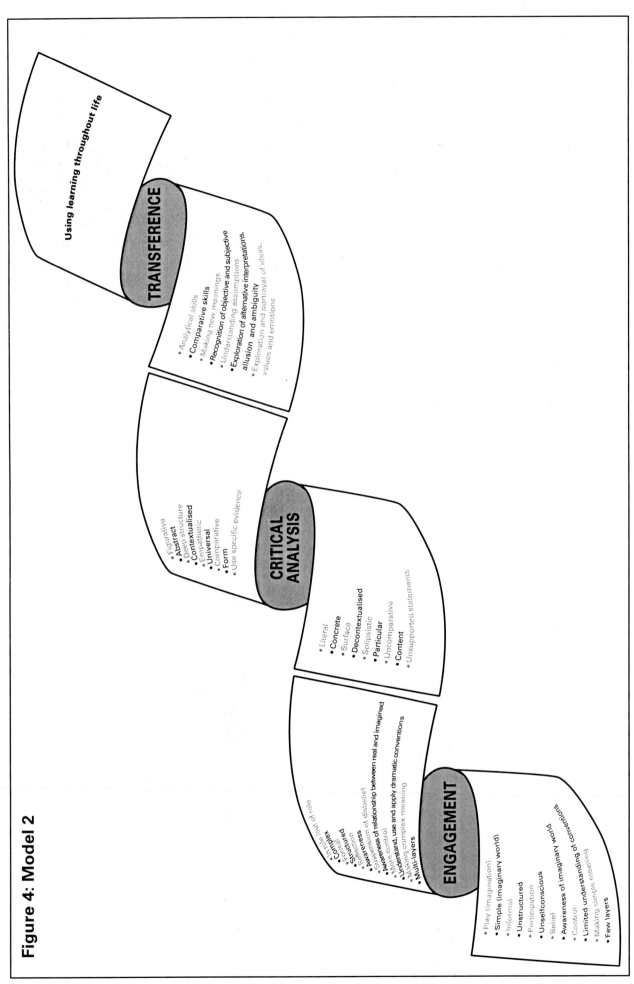

Using learning throughout life

TRANSFERENCE

* Analytical skills
* Comparative skills
* Making new meanings
* Recognition of objective and subjective
* Understanding of alternative interpretations,
* Exploration of alternative interpretations,
  allusion and ambiguity
* Exploration and portrayal of ideas,
  values and emotions

* Figurative
* Abstract
* Deep structure
* Contextualised
* Empathetic
* Universal
* Comparative
* Form
* Use specific evidence

CRITICAL ANALYSIS

* Literal
* Concrete
* Surface
* Decontextualised
* Solipsistic
* Particular
* Uncomparative
* Content
* Unsupported statements

* In and out of role
* Complex
* Formal
* Structured
* Reflection
* Awareness
* Suspension of disbelief
* Awareness of relationship between real and imagined
* More control
* Understand, use and apply dramatic conventions
* Making complex meaning
* Multi-layers

ENGAGEMENT

* Play (imagination)
* Simple (imaginary world)
* Informal
* Unstructured
* Participation
* Unselfconscious
* Belief
* Awareness of imaginary world
* Control
* Limited understanding of conventions
* Making simple meaning
* Few layers

Unit 1
Drama to support text and sentence level objectives in the Literacy Hour

The approaches outlined below give pupils an opportunity to use drama strategies to explore a written text. Through structured sessions they are encouraged to use contextual clues to predict story endings and increase their awareness of the use of verb tenses in narrative. By using drama to support text and sentence level objectives in the Literacy Hour, pupils develop critical awareness and higher order reading skills of inference and deduction, using evidence from the text.

Resources

A copy of *Farmer Duck* by Martin Waddell and Helen Oxenbury (Walker Big Books, 1991)

A puppet or soft toy to represent a duck

A 'newspaper article' about the duck (see example)

A flipchart and pen

An outline of Farmer Duck drawn on a large sheet of paper, under the heading 'Farmer Duck'

Post-its

Learning objectives

These sessions follow the structure of the Literacy Hour and show how drama can be used to support the objectives. A number of strategies are described that are used here to explore *Farmer Duck*, but can in fact be transferred to other written texts.

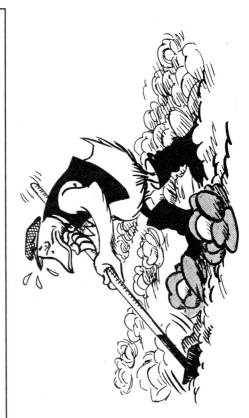

Extracts from the units …

Write the word 'hardworking' on a Post-It label and place this on the sheet of paper with the outline of the duck. Ask the class to explain what this word means and why you have put it on the sheet. Draw the pupils' attention to the fact that the duck is hardworking by referring to all the jobs he did in the story. Ask the pupils if they can think of one or two more words to describe the duck, e.g. sad/tired/kind. Write these on Post-its and add to the sheet. Explain that you will be recording more information about the character of Farmer Duck on the role on the wall during the week. Make it clear that they will find out more about his character by reading the book.

Commentary

The pupils add words or phrases to the role on the wall to focus their attention on the character of the duck as they read the story. Using Post-its enables them to add or delete words in the light of further information from the book. Having a role on the wall also serves as a reference point for writing. This strategy is also useful for demonstrating how a character can change during the course of a story.

(All NC references are to the programmes of study at KS1.)

NLS/NC REFERENCES	ACTIVITIES AND APPROACHES	TEACHING AND LEARNING COMMENTARY

ACTIVITIES AND APPROACHES

Session one

Shared reading

NLS Y2 T2: T6

NC En1 Speaking: 1a,b,d

Drama: 4a

- Keep the book hidden.
- Ask the pupils if they will pretend to help a character from this week's big book.
- Show the pupils the duck and make it look sad.
- Explain that the duck is the main character in the story.
- Ask them how they think the duck is feeling.
- Explain that the duck is shy and will only talk to the pupils via whispering to you.

Ask the duck why he looks so sad. Let the duck whisper in your ear to reveal that he is very tired because he has to do all the work on the farm.

Ask the duck what kind of jobs he has to do. When the duck whispers an answer, make the jobs match the ones carried out by Farmer Duck in the story. Let the duck ask the pupils if they will help with some of the jobs, whilst he has a rest. Then put the duck down as if to sleep.

NLS Y2 T2: S5

NC En1 Speaking:1d

Listening: 2c

Drama: 4a

Explain that everyone will need to pretend to do the jobs. Ask the pupils to recall the jobs mentioned by the duck and make a list on the board using the present tense for the verbs, e.g. *dig* the potatoes, *pick* the apples. Make sure the pupils understand what each job entails and offer brief explanations where necessary.

Before miming the jobs, agree on a suitable mimed action for each job. Choose simple actions that are suited to the available space. For example, bringing the animals in from the fields might be represented by pretending to open a gate or a barn door and picking apples might involve reaching up high to pick the apples and then miming putting them in a basket.

NLS Y2 T2: S5

NC En1 Listening: 2a

Drama: 4a

Using the list as a guide, perform the jobs in order, using and emphasising the present tense of the verbs, e.g. 'First we need to *dig* the potatoes ... now we need to...'. Perform each action in unison, as a class. Spend enough time on each job to make it feel like a chore, but not so long that the pupils lose interest.

NLS Y2 T2: T4

NC En1 Speaking: 1a,b,c,d

Listening: 2a,b,c

Drama: 4a

After completing the jobs, talk about how hard the jobs are and mention that the duck may become ill as a result. Ask the pupils what they think the duck should do to solve his problem. Mention the farmer being lazy and the duck having nowhere else to live. Accept all reasonable suggestions and discuss the possible consequences of each idea. Show the pupils the cover of the

TEACHING AND LEARNING COMMENTARY

Puppet in role

The pupils quickly engage with the main character in the book by being introduced to a puppet who plays the role of the main character. Focusing on Farmer Duck before introducing the pupils to the book will help them become more aware of the character when they come to read the book and will help them see the unfolding events from his perspective.

Mantle of the expert

In session one, the pupils are put into a position of high status, as people capable of carrying out a range of farm jobs. This increases their desire to become involved.

The pupils are also treated as experts when they are invited to speculate on how to solve the duck's problems. This prepares the pupils for the part of the story where they will be asked to predict what the farm animals plan to do to help the duck.

In session four, the pupils become experts in the truth about the duck and this motivates them to help the teacher write a letter to the newspaper.

Occupational mime

In session one, the pupils experience the hardships faced by the main character through representing the work in mime. This physical act helps the pupils relate to, and later recall, the hardships faced by the duck. It also provides a more meaningful context for written work.

Cracking Drama © NATE Drama Committee 2000

NC/NLS REFERENCES

NLS Y2 T2: S5

NC En3 Language structure: 7b

ACTIVITIES AND APPROACHES

Farmer Duck big book and explain that they will find out what happened to the duck when they start to read the book tomorrow.

Suggestions for related independent tasks

1 Farmer Jill's Busy Day

Give pupils a passage on a farming theme containing some of the phrases on the board and ask them to write in the missing words, e.g.

Yesterday Farmer Jill had a busy day. First, she _ the animals and then she _ the vegetables. Later she _ some seeds in the fields and then _ her dinner. She _ very tired after dinner ... at night she _ so tired that she _ to bed early.

Choose the missing words from this list: feed/fed/dug/dig/planted/plant/eat/ ate ... etc.

2 Verb tense Snap

Give pairs of pupils a list of ten verbs in the present tense, together with their past tense equivalents. Try to give each pair a slightly different list. Give each pair ten small white cards and ten in another colour. Each pair should write the present tense of a verb on a white card and the past tense of the same verb on a coloured card to form pairs. Alternatively, the cards could be ready written. They should then mix up the cards and deal them out to play a Snap type game, shouting 'Snap!' when they match a present tense verb card with its past tense equivalent. Pairs should play the game two or three times before exchanging their sets of Snap cards with those of other pairs, so that they can play the game with a set of different verbs.

Plenary session

Ask some of the pupils who carried out task 2 to read out one or two of the verbs on their white cards and ask the pupils who did not carry out this task to guess what the matching past tense Snap card would be.

NLS Y2 T2: T6

NC En1 Speaking: 1b
       Listening: 2c
       Drama: 4a

Write the word 'hardworking' on a Post-it label and place this on the sheet of paper with the outline of the duck. Ask the class to explain what this word means and why you have put it on the sheet. Draw the pupils' attention to the fact that the duck is hardworking by referring to all the jobs he did in the story. Ask the pupils if they can think of one or two more words to describe the duck, e.g. sad/tired/kind. Write these on Post-its and add to the sheet. Explain that you will be recording more information about the character of Farmer Duck on the role on the wall during the week. Make it clear that they will find out more about his character by reading the book.

TEACHING AND LEARNING COMMENTARY

Role on the wall

The pupils add words or phrases to the role on the wall to focus their attention on the character of the duck as they read the story. Using Post-its enables them to add or delete words in the light of further information from the book. Having a role on the wall also serves as a reference point for writing. This strategy is also useful for demonstrating how a character can change during the course of a story.

NC/NLS REFERENCES

NLS   Y2 T2: T6
NC   En1 Group discussion and
              interaction: 3a,b,e
       En2 Literature: 3a

NLS   Y2 T2: T4
NC   En1 Group discussion and
              interaction: 3
       En2 Literature: 3b,c,f

NLS   Y2 T2: S5
NC   En2 Reading strategies: 1h,n

NLS   Y2 T2: T4
NC   En1 Speaking: 8d
              Listening: 9a
              Group discussion and
              interaction: 10b

NLS   Y2 T2: S5
NC   En1 Standard English: 5

NLS   Y2 T2: T6
NC   En1 Group discussion and
              interaction: 10b

ACTIVITIES AND APPROACHES

Further developments for sessions two to five

Session two: shared reading

Read and discuss the book, up to the point where the animals make a plan. Draw the pupils' attention to how the jobs have been recorded and illustrated and ask the pupils if they would like to add any more words to describe the character of the duck on the role on the wall.

Remind the pupils about the advice they gave the duck in session one and invite them to predict what the animals plan to do.

Session two: sentence level

Cover some of the verbs in the story so far with Post-its. Write the present tense of the verb on the Post-it and invite the pupils to guess what the past tense will be in the story. Pick out any patterns such as '-ed' words. Distribute the Post-Its among a few pupils and ask them to put them back on the correct verbs.

Session two: suggestions for independent tasks

Ask groups to work in pairs to write their two best predictions about what the animals will do in the story and what the consequences will be.

Session two: plenary

Ask the class to listen for verbs in the past tense, as some pupils read out their predictions. This should make the point that predictions are in the future tense.

Session three: shared reading

Read and discuss the rest of the book with the class to discover the animals' plan. Then discuss what the duck is like and add other words or phrases to the role on the wall, e.g. scared of the farmer / is liked by the other animals / happy / pleased to see the farmer go / relieved … etc.

Session four: shared writing

Bring back the puppet or toy duck and make it look sad. Express surprise that the duck is sad now that the farmer has been thrown out. Let the duck show you a newspaper report saying the following:

TEACHING AND LEARNING COMMENTARY

Poor farmer thrown out by lazy duck

A lazy duck and his animal friends have thrown a poor farmer out of his own farm. The farmer told our reporter that the lazy duck stayed in bed all day eating chocolates whilst the farmer did all the work on the farm and all the ironing and all the cooking and cleaning in the house. Last week the cruel duck forced the other animals to throw the farmer out. If YOU know any thing about this selfish duck please write to us.

Let the duck ask the pupils to write to the newspaper and tell them the truth.

Put the duck away after promising to help. Before starting to compose a letter to the newspaper, use the text in the book and the list of jobs that the pupils carried out for the duck to check what the duck did on the farm. Stress the need to change the words on the list into the past tense and put them into a sentence for the letter to the newspaper, e.g. '*the duck dug the vegetables*' instead of '*dig the vegetables*'. Also, compare the words describing the duck in the newspaper to those on the role on the wall. Decide on an appropriate tone for the letter and make a rough draft.

NLS Y2 T2: S5; T6,12,14

NC En3 Composition: 1
Planning and drafting: 2
Language structure: 7
Breadth of study: 9, 11

Writing in role

In session four the pupils are invited to help the teacher compose a letter to an imaginary newspaper as if the events in the story were true. In this sense they are writing in the role of friends of the duck, who initially helped him with his jobs and gave him advice on how to solve his problems. The imaginary context provides a vehicle for writing. It gives the pupils a reason to examine the text and an incentive to write about the character of the duck.

Session four: sentence level

Edit and proof-read the letter – check the spelling, verb tenses and other transcriptional points relevant to the needs of the class. Bring back the duck so that the class can read the letter to him. Make the duck look pleased but, if appropriate, you can make the duck point out any parts of the letter that are unclear or do not make sense.

NLS Y2 T2: S5, T12

NC En3 Punctuation: 3
Spelling: 4
Language structure: 7
Breadth of study: 11

Session five: shared reading/writing

Bring the duck back to thank the pupils for helping him. Explain that the letter went into the newspaper and now everyone knows that the farmer was telling lies. Let the duck ask the pupils to read *Farmer Duck* to him one last time before he leaves. Reflect on the story and how it portrays the characters of the duck and the farmer through words and illustrations. Write a role on the wall for the farmer and compare it to the one for the duck.

NLS Y2 T2: T6

NC En1 Drama: 4a
En2 Literature: 3a
Literature: 6e

Unit 2

Drama to support text work in the Literacy Hour (nursery rhymes)

During this structured session, pupils are familiarised with the traditional rhyme 'Humpty Dumpty'. They explore the written text through drama and develop critical awareness of character and situation in text.

Resources

A large copy of the nursery rhyme 'Humpty Dumpty'

One simple costume for each of the characters in the rhyme, e.g. a bright scarf for Humpty, coats worn over the shoulders for the king's men and a paper crown or a cloak for the king

A low table or bench covered with dark material, to represent the wall

Five A4-sized star shapes, cut from or drawn onto white card

A thick felt pen in a bright colour

Learning objectives

A traditional nursery rhyme 'Humpty Dumpty' is explored through the use of drama activities, within the structure of the Literacy Hour.

Extracts from the units …

Choose a few pupils to be the king's men and one child to be the king. Explain that this picture will show the king's men trying to put Humpty together. If the pupils would like to include the horses, remind them that the king's men were probably not on horseback during this moment.

Commentary:
Frame three is discussed in more detail and may be more suitable for Year 1. With younger pupils this frame could be worked on as a separate lesson or the line could be recited without the freeze-frame to complete the rhyme.

NLS/NC REFERENCES

ACTIVITIES AND APPROACHES

TEACHING AND LEARNING COMMENTARY

Session outline

Shared reading (approximately 15 mins) of the text 'Humpty Dumpty': sit the pupils near enough to see the copy of the rhyme but allow space for a small group to stand at the front.

Read the rhyme to the pupils and encourage them to join in as you point to the words.

Ask the pupils if some of them will pretend to be in some pictures of the rhyme, like freeze-frames on a video.

Emphasise that they will need to be very good at keeping still.

Put out the costumes and props and explain who and what they are to represent. Explain that the stars will be used later on, so that how the people in the pictures might be feeling.

NLS YR: T7. Y1 T2: T7
NC   En1 Group discussion and interaction: 3a,e

Drama: 4a
Group discussion and interaction: 10b
Drama activities: 11b
En2 Literature: 3a,d,f

Frame one: 'Humpty Dumpty sat on a wall'

Choose one child to represent Humpty Dumpty as he sits on the wall. Ask the child to put on the costume to signify the character. Explain that this picture will be about the first line of the rhyme.

Ask the class to read this line with you. Then ask the class if they think Humpty should be smiling as he sits on the wall or should he look unhappy. Speculate about why Humpty may have decided to sit there and whether he knew that he might fall. Talk about how Humpty Dumpty might be feeling.

Ask for a word, or words, to describe how Humpty might be feeling, e.g. happy, sad, scared, brave. Select a word based on what most of the class say and then write the word inside one of the stars. Emphasise that the star tells us how people feel. Ask the class to repeat the word on the card.

Ask the class to use their faces to show how Humpty might look if he was feeling this way. When the class have decided on Humpty's facial expression, let everyone practise making the appropriate expression when you hold up the star.

Now ask Humpty to sit on the wall and wait for the word 'Freeze' before making the picture. Humpty should hold still in freeze as the class say the first line. Repeat this again, but this time encourage the class to recite the line as if they were feeling like Humpty. Let one child hold up the star during the freeze-frame, to remind everyone of the appropriate feeling. Tell the pupils that these pretending pictures are called freeze-frames.

NLS Y1 T1: T11
NC   En2 Literature: 3f

Introducing freeze-frames and feelings stars

Young pupils will feel more secure if given a brief but clear outline of what is about to happen. They are introduced to the concept of a freeze-frame and given a brief explanation of the function of the feelings stars.

Making a contract

In being asked to pretend that some pupils might be part of a picture of the rhyme, the pupils have effectively been asked to enter into an informal contract to imagine that the characters and situation in the rhyme are real. This facilitates the discussion of characters' feelings later in the lesson.

Freeze-frames provide a visual focus for reflection and analysis. They bring the rhyme to life for the pupils so that it jumps off the page. Freeze-frames also encourage the pupils to view the incident in the rhyme from the perspectives of the different characters and to consider each character's feelings. This strategy can be adapted to focus on any significant moment or moments from other rhymes, stories or narrative poems.

The feelings stars help to reinforce the feelings and introduce appropriate written vocabulary. Young pupils who can talk about characters' feelings and motives in stories and rhymes are likely to find it easier to write about characters in essays and comprehension tests when they are older. This strategy helps to develop early skills of critical analysis with regard to written texts.

The way the freeze-frames are negotiated with the class represents an interactive and inclusive whole class strategy. The responsibility for the moment lies with the class and not just the performers. This approach is a basic form of forum theatre.

Note: Extra characters can be included in the freeze-frames, such as the queen or the person who built the wall.

NC/NLS REFERENCES

ACTIVITIES AND APPROACHES

TEACHING AND LEARNING COMMENTARY

Frame two: 'Humpty Dumpty had a great fall'

NLS YR T7. Y1 T2: T7, T11
NC En1 Group discussion and interaction: 3a,e
　　Drama: 4a
　　Group discussion and interaction: 10b
　　Drama activities: 11b
　En2 Literature: 3a,d,f

This can be a picture of Humpty after he has fallen off the wall or just as he is about to fall. Ask the class to suggest a word to write in Humpty's second 'feelings star', as he lies on the ground.

When you have written the word in the star, ask Humpty and the class to make the appropriate expression, as before. Repeat the procedures as in frame one, to make a freeze-frame of the second line, as the pupils recite it.

If the pupils already have a clear understanding of freeze-frames and feelings stars, this section may be quicker than frame one and the class could move on to include a third frame.

Frame three (optional): 'All the king's horses and all the king's men / Couldn't put Humpty together again'

NLS YR: T7

Choose a few pupils to be the king's men and one child to be the king. Explain that this picture will show the king's men trying to put Humpty together. If the pupils would like to include the horses, remind them that the king's men were probably not on horseback during this moment.

Frame three is discussed in more detail and may be more suitable for Year 1. With younger pupils this frame could be worked on as a separate lesson or the line could be recited without the freeze-frame to complete the rhyme.

NLS Y1 T1: T7
NC En1 Group discussion and interaction: 3a,b,c,d,e
　　Drama: 4a
　　Listening: 9a
　　Group discussion and interaction: 10b
　　Drama activities: 11b
　En2 Literature: 3a

In this frame, ask the class to make decisions on where and how the men should be positioned and where the king might be. Give them some options, such as 'Do you think the king was watching from a window in his castle or was he somewhere else?' If the class decide that the king was in another place, such as his castle, he can be positioned at the side of the main freeze-frame.

Ask the pupils to think about the relationship between Humpty and the king; ask them to speculate on why Humpty sat on the wall and why the king should try to help. Talk about how the king might have been feeling and write a word in a star. Then ask them how the men might have been feeling and write a star for them as a group. Suggest some possibilities other than 'sad', such as 'worried', 'tired' or 'angry' (with Humpty for sitting on the wall or with the king for asking them to do an impossible job).

When the words have been written in the stars, hold them up and ask the class to demonstrate the appropriate facial expressions. Then ask the pupils playing the king and his men to take up their frozen positions as the class recite the last two lines. Before they begin, ask the class how they feel about the incident and suggest that this time they might recite the lines to express their own feelings. Let some pupils hold up the stars near the appropriate characters during the freeze.

NLS Y1 T1: T11
NC En2 Group discussion and interaction: 3d

Read the rhyme again without the freeze-frames. Then ask some pupils to hold up the stars. Ask the class if they can remember whom each star belonged to and when each character felt that way in the rhyme.

Unit 3
Drama as a holding form for literacy and speaking and listening

This lesson is intended to be linked to a number of Literacy Hours to support NLS objectives. Further activities are suggested at the end that could be spread over several lessons. Pupils may read the texts above or write items for a role-play or display area such as a Visitors' Centre for Sunny Valley.

Resources

A choice of text examples:

- non-fiction – brochures and guides to national parks, nature reserves and places of outstanding natural beauty

- fiction – *Dinosaurs and All That Rubbish* by Michael Foreman and *The Paper Bag Prince* by Colin Thompson (Dragonfly, 1997)

A large sketch map placed on a moveable easel or board

One or two blue PE mats for lessons in the hall

A felt pen and a whistle

Music to represent the morning (optional), e.g. *Dawn is a Feeling* by The Moody Blues

A scarf or an imaginary letter from a visitor

A related fictional text (optional – see text examples)

Learning objectives

A number of drama strategies are used to give pupils an opportunity to explore issues and read and write within a dramatic context. The session provides a stimulus that motivates and supports pupils to write for a wide range of purposes related to a common theme or issue.

Extracts from the units ...

Tell the pupils that the drama will be about an imaginary place called Sunny Valley. Explain that Sunny Valley is a beautiful place, which attracts many visitors. It is very popular with children as well as with adults.

Using the map, point out the river and other features. Ask the pupils to imagine that the hall represents Sunny Valley for the purposes of the drama.

Commentary:
Through whole group drama, the teacher can create life-like situations that encourage motivation and commitment, stimulate language and enhance learning.

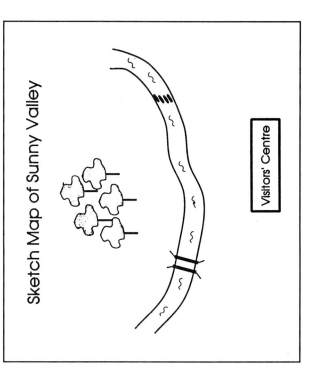

Sketch Map of Sunny Valley

Visitors' Centre

| NLS/NC REFERENCES | ACTIVITIES AND APPROACHES | TEACHING AND LEARNING COMMENTARY |

ACTIVITIES AND APPROACHES

The lesson (in the hall)

Preparation

Place the mats lengthways across the middle of the hall to represent the area of the river between the bridge and the stepping stones on the map (see page 28).

Place a copy of the map in the hall on the easel.

Organisation

Organise the pupils to sit with their partners but in a whole group. They should sit along one side of the hall facing the mats, as if they are sitting in the Visitors' Centre on the map. Place the map where all the pupils can see it. This can be moved later if it obscures their view of the mats.

Introducing the imaginary place

Tell the pupils that the drama will be about an imaginary place called Sunny Valley. Explain that Sunny Valley is a beautiful place, which attracts many visitors. It is very popular with children as well as with adults.

Using the map, point out the river and other features. Ask the pupils to imagine that the hall represents Sunny Valley for the purposes of the drama.

Defining the space

Ask the pupils to imagine that the mats represent the river, between the bridge and the stepping stones. Ask them to imagine that the river extends to either side of the mats. Indicate the parts of the hall that will represent the rest of the river.

Use mime to demonstrate how people can cross the river in two places; by walking over the imaginary bridge or by jumping over the imaginary stepping stones. Make it clear that the crossing areas are on the hall floor and not actually on the mats. Stress that no one is to step on or touch the mats in the drama.

Point out the area of the woods behind the river by referring to the map in relation to the hall. Explain that when the drama starts, the area in which the pupils are now sitting will become the Visitors' Centre.

Define any areas of the hall that are out of bounds for the drama, such as the wall bars or behind the piano.

NC   En1 Drama: 4a
      Drama activities: 11a

TEACHING AND LEARNING COMMENTARY

Whole group drama

This strategy involves all the pupils, and sometimes the teacher, behaving and responding as if they were living through the drama in reality. All responses should be appropriate to the dramatic context. It is important to ask pupils for their agreement to take part in this imaginary situation. This constitutes a kind of contract to behave appropriately in the drama. Most pupils enjoy drama and can often appreciate the need for a shared agreement of this kind. The majority of pupils will accept this contract, providing everything is explained clearly and presented in a positive manner. A firm, clear but positive introduction works to reassure those pupils who might otherwise be reluctant to participate. If clear signals are incorporated into the introduction to the drama then it should be a straightforward process to stop the drama if pupils break the contract and behave inappropriately. Pupils should be asked to sit at the side of the room if they refuse to comply with the contract.

Through whole group drama, the teacher can create life-like situations that encourage motivation and commitment, stimulate language and enhance learning.

24

NC/NLS REFERENCES

NC   En1   Group discussion and interaction: 3a, 10b

ACTIVITIES AND APPROACHES

Creating the imaginary place

Tell the pupils that you would like them to add more things to Sunny Valley before the drama starts. Working in their groups of three, each group is asked to think of one thing that they would like to add to Sunny Valley. They are also asked to decide where they would like their choice to be located, both on the map and in the hall. Explain that they can choose something that grows, or they can choose living things such as plants or animals or perhaps a building for people to use. Make it clear that anything will be accepted, as long as they feel it would fit into a place like Sunny Valley. Some classes may need to be warned that anything inappropriate will not be accepted. Give the pupils a few minutes to complete the task and ask them to fold their arms as a sign that their group is ready.

Ask groups to take turns to state their choice and then sit in the equivalent place in the hall to where they would like their choice to be located: for example, if a group chose a park near the river, they would sit beside the mats. As each group states their choice and walk into the hall, record their item on the map in words or using a symbol.

When everyone's choice has been recorded on the map, ask the class to sit back in their original positions in the Visitors' Centre. Check the map with the class to see if everything has been correctly recorded and located. No more additions should be allowed from this point on, unless they are minor adaptations to the original choices.

Preparing to work in role

Ask the pupils to play the roles of some of the visitors to Sunny Valley. Refer to the map and discuss some of the activities they might pursue as visitors. Demonstrate and discuss how some of these activities might be mimed for the drama, e.g. climbing mountains, swimming in the river or playing football. Anticipate any potentially boisterous interpretations and set clear rules beforehand, e.g. swimming in the river should avoid the mat areas and perhaps involve walking whilst miming swimming strokes rather than lying on the floor.

Give groups a few minutes to decide on two suitable activities they will engage in when they play the roles of visitors and ask them to fold their arms as a sign that they have completed the task.

NC   En1   Drama: 4a,c

Explain that the drama will start with a freeze-frame of the moment when they were just about to start their first activity in Sunny Valley. This can be compared to a freeze-frame on a video. Give groups a few minutes to decide where they will be located in the freeze-frame and how their bodies will be positioned. Tell them to fold their arms when they have decided.

TEACHING AND LEARNING COMMENTARY

Creating the place provides a sense of shared ownership that facilitates motivation to participate.

Beginning a whole group drama with freeze-frames helps to focus thinking and provides a clear, thoughtful and controlled start to the activity.

NC/NLS REFERENCES

ACTIVITIES AND APPROACHES

Make it clear that when they come to life, they should speak to each other as if they really were the visitors. Ask the class for some examples of what they might talk about.

Place the map in the Visitors' Centre as a prop, making it clear that no one must touch or mark it.

Explain that the drama will start when you say the word 'Action' and stop when you say the word 'Freeze' and blow the whistle.

Ask the groups to walk into their freeze positions a few at a time until everyone is frozen.

Dramatic play

NC   En1   Drama: 4a,b,c
      Drama activities: 11a

Wait for everyone to keep still and then say 'Action' to start the drama. Let this run for a few minutes or for as long as most pupils appear to be absorbed in the activities.

Stop the action by blowing the whistle and saying 'Freeze' and ask the groups to return to their original places in the Visitors' Centre area, a few at a time.

Acting for an audience

NC   En1   Drama: 4d
      Drama activities: 11c

Select half the class to return to their original freeze-frame positions in the hall and, on the word 'Action', ask them to show the rest of the class some of the activities they had been doing. Ask them to provide a shortened approximate version to show as many different activities as possible in a few minutes. The audience should be asked to guess the activities after the performance. Then the audience is given a turn to perform their activities in the same way.

TEACHING AND LEARNING COMMENTARY

If this kind of work is new to the pupils, they may take a while before they feel confident enough to speak to each other in role. This usually improves after a few minutes, but if they remain very quiet for a long time or find the silence embarrassing, freeze the drama and make suggestions about what they could talk about before asking them to find someone to talk to when the drama restarts. If they are still quiet it is best to carry on to the next section.

Most pupils enjoy this kind of activity and take part sensibly, but pupils who persist in misbehaving should be withdrawn and asked to watch until they feel they can take part in an acceptable way.

It is best to keep the guessing sections fairly brief, but they do provide an opportunity to point out and encourage imaginative mime and interesting conversations in drama.

The audience should be asked to pick out any aspects of the performances that they liked. This introduces pupils to the idea of positive criticism of other people's drama work. Any negative comments on individual acting should be discouraged at this stage in the interests of building confidence.

NC/NLS REFERENCES

NC   En1 Drama: 4a,b,c
              Drama activities: 11a

ACTIVITIES AND APPROACHES

Taking on roles of responsibility

Ask the pupils to take on new roles as the owners of Sunny Valley who work there to look after the place. Explain that when the drama starts again they should imagine that it is the start of their working day. Music can be played to provide atmosphere, if available. Explain that, as workers, they will need to get everything ready for when the visitors arrive later in the morning.

Show the pupils the map and ask them to suggest what kind of jobs they will have to do. These might include feeding animals, making sandwiches in a café, gardening or cleaning. Ask them to imagine that there are a number of sheds around Sunny Valley containing any equipment they may need.

Give groups a few minutes to decide on two jobs they will do when the drama starts and tell them to fold their arms when they have decided.

Explain that you will say 'Action' to start the drama and then point to groups a few at a time to imagine that they have just arrived in the morning to start work. They should carry on with the jobs and find more until you blow the whistle and say 'Freeze' to stop the drama. Let this run for a few minutes or for as long as most pupils appear to be absorbed in the work.

After stopping the drama ask the pupils to return to the Visitors' Centre area a few at a time.

Reflection

Ask the pupils what they liked best and least about working in Sunny Valley. Ask them what they feel is the most popular attraction for visitors. Ask them how they might like to improve the existing facilities. Conclude the drama.

Further work

The work may be extended through creating a Visitors' Centre display area in the classroom consisting of maps, directions, brochures, leaflets, etc. to fit in with NLS objectives on non-fiction writing. Letters of complaint on issues such as litter can be delivered to Sunny Valley workers. These require a written response, composed in the Literacy Hour.

TEACHING AND LEARNING COMMENTARY

Inside the drama, the pupils can take on a variety of different roles, including adult roles of responsibility such as owners of Sunny Valley. Such roles give pupils a sense of ownership over the drama and have the potential to engage pupils in problem-solving and negotiating solutions to real-life issues.

Pupils are encouraged to form opinions about their roles of responsibility through reflecting on the service they provide. This reinforces their roles for the follow-on.

NC   En1 Group discussion and
              interaction: 3a,b,c,d
              Drama: 4a,b,c
              Group discussion and
              interaction: 10c
              Drama activities: 11a

NLS Y3 T2: T16
       Y4 T1: T26
       Y4 T3: T25
       Y6 T1: T22

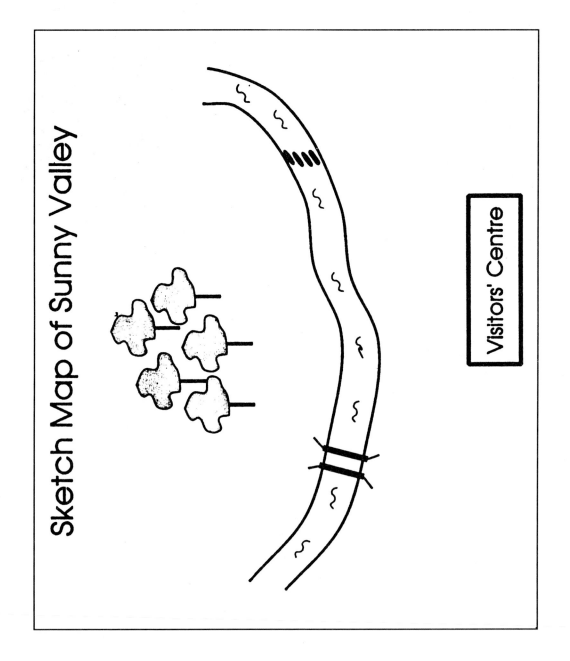

Sketch Map of Sunny Valley

Visitors' Centre

Unit 4
Using drama as a visual focus for reflection and analysis of text

Pupils are given opportunities to use drama to explore, and develop their critical analysis of, a text.

Resources

A copy of the poem 'Matilda' by Hilaire Belloc, preferably with illustrations (e.g. the version illustrated by Posy Simmonds published by Red Fox Picture Books)

At least one copy of the text of the poem per group

A scarf to represent Matilda

A cardboard thought bubble

Blackboard or flipchart and pen

Learning objectives

The lesson described illustrates how drama activities can be used to explore the poem 'Matilda'. It is not intended to take place in the Literacy Hour, but aspects could be adapted to fit into shared reading sessions. If the lesson is linked to Literacy Hours, it has the potential to fulfil a number of NLS objectives.

Extracts from the units ...

Give each group a copy of the poem and allocate one to four lines to each group. Not all lines need be represented. Give groups a time limit and offer support where needed.

Each group will then present their frame and thoughts to the rest of the class as you read the lines. Let the class read in any lines that have not been represented by a freeze-frame.

Commentary:
Modelling and giving examples help pupils when they come to interpret lines in groups.

(All NC references are for the programmes of study at KS2.)

NC/NLS REFERENCES	ACTIVITIES AND APPROACHES	TEACHING AND LEARNING COMMENTARY
	The lesson	
	Introduction	
NLS Y3 T3: T5 Y5 T2: T4	Read the poem to the pupils without showing them the illustrations. Explain that you would like them to illustrate the poem using freeze-frames. If this strategy is new to the pupils it can be compared to a pause on a video. The pupils must represent the people in a frozen moment, to illustrate different parts of the poem. Explain that each group will eventually be given a few lines from the poem to illustrate in a freeze-frame with spoken thoughts. They must try to include all the group in some capacity and can invent extra characters if they wish.	Freeze-frames act as a visual focus for discussion and analysis of the poem and help pupils to visualise the text. The pupils must also strive to understand the meaning of the lines in order to make a meaningful visual representation.
	Forum theatre	
	Work out the first frame in the following way with the whole class first, as an example.	Forum theatre involves all the class in a discussion of the opening lines. This acts as a demonstration of the small group task, but it also provides an opportunity to ask probing questions that investigate the text. If the class finds group work difficult, all the freeze-frames could be worked out and performed as a class, using forum theatre.
	Write up the first two lines of the poem on the board:	
	Matilda told such dreadful lies, *It made one gasp and stretch one's eyes;*	
NLS Y4 T2: T6 NC En1 Drama: 4c Drama activities: 11a	Ask the whole class what these lines mean and refer to archaic language if appropriate. Discuss how they might illustrate these lines in a frozen moment known as a freeze-frame. Demonstrate by using pupils from one of the groups to play the parts of the people in the freeze-frame. Negotiate an appropriate context and setting for the freeze-frame and decide on the characters. Then go through each character in turn and ask members of the class to decide where these characters are likely to be looking and why. Encourage close reference to the lines and use this as an opportunity to discuss the implications of the phrase 'stretch one's eyes'. Talk about each character's feelings and expressions and introduce an awareness of audience by asking questions such as 'Can we make it look more interesting?' and 'Can the audience see everyone's face?'.	
	Ask the pupils to check that the freeze-frame is a good representation of the lines before asking them to work out what each character might have been thinking. Do this by holding the cardboard thought bubble over each of the character's heads in turn and asking the class to suggest appropriate thoughts. Let the pupils playing the characters have the final decision on what they are thinking.	Considering characters' thoughts and speaking thoughts aloud help pupils to see moments from the characters' perspectives.

NC/NLS REFERENCES

ACTIVITIES AND APPROACHES

TEACHING AND LEARNING COMMENTARY

Explain that when you say the word 'Freeze' the characters must stand still whilst someone reads out the lines. Then, when you say the word 'Thoughts', they must speak out their thoughts in a pre-arranged order. They must maintain the freeze whilst speaking the thoughts and remain still to the count of five after the last thought.

NLS   Y4 T2: T5
NLS   Y5 T2: T5
NC   En1 Drama: 4a,c
            Speaking: 8a
       Drama activities: 11a

Perform the freeze-frame as agreed. Then explain that each group will be given a few lines to use as a basis for a similar freeze-frame with thoughts. Go through each group's lines briefly and ask the class for suggestions on how they might be interpreted. Use this as an opportunity to explain any figurative language or difficult words and to point out any examples of archaic language.

Modelling and giving examples help pupils when they come to interpret lines in groups.

Give each group a copy of the poem and allocate one to four lines to each group. Not all lines need be represented. Give groups a time limit and offer support where needed.

Each group will then present their frame and thoughts to the rest of the class as you read the lines. Let the class read in any lines that have not been represented by a freeze-frame.

NLS   Y4 T2: T6
NC   En1 Drama: 4c,d
       Drama activities: 11a

After the freeze-frames, mention any examples of good practice with regard to interesting interpretations or imaginative thoughts and point out the interpretations of any archaic or figurative language. Invite comments from pupils on examples of good practice.

Identifying good practice helps pupils to improve their own work in the future.

Older pupils may be able to follow this by considering a more abstract, symbolic, class freeze-frame to represent the theme of the poem as a cautionary tale about lying. For example, they may be asked to make a group into an imaginary statue to commemorate Matilda's story.

Follow-up work

After the drama, ask the pupils to illustrate the poem using drawings and thought bubbles. Give the pupils a few lines each to copy out and illustrate. Finally, show the pupils the illustrations from the published poem and invite comparisons with their own attempts.

This creates a link between the pupils' attempts to represent the text visually and the work of an illustrator.

Unit 5
Drama to motivate and enhance text level work in the Literacy Hour

These activities are designed to be completed during the Literacy Hour over a period of one week, but can be adapted to cover a longer period and some of the activities can be carried out during a longer period over a period of one week, but can be adapted to cover a longer period and some of the activities can be carried out during extended writing. The activities for shared reading and writing are designed to take place with the whole class, during the first 15 to 20 minutes of the Literacy Hour. The independent activities are designed for pupils who are working independently of the teacher, whilst she/he works with a group on guided reading or writing.

Resources for session one

Text extracts from:

Beowulf by Charles Keeping and Kevin Crossley-Holland (OUP, 1982)

Beowulf Dragon Slayer by Rosemary Sutcliff (Heinemann, 1961)

Beowulf: A verse translation by Michael Alexander (Penguin,1973)

An enlarged copy or individual photocopies of the blurb on each book.

A cloak (or the background to the story of *Beowulf* written on a scroll)

A flip chart and pen

Learning objectives

Pupils are given opportunities to use dramatic techniques to explore texts. In doing so, they are familiarised with the content and style of a traditional saga as well as being motivated and supported to make comparisons between different authors' treatment of the same story. The writing of the blurb encourages them to develop persuasive and informative writing.

Extracts from the units ...

Ask the class to imagine that they had all carried out a brave deed as a group of warriors on an expedition. Decide on what this will be and work together to write a summary of this to read out chorally to Beowulf during the role-play. This will be read out in addition to the pupils' own summaries.

Commentary:
Shared writing provides a model for pupils' own work and a finished summary as a safety net to use in the role-play, should pupils not complete many of their own.

NC/NLS REFERENCES

ACTIVITIES AND APPROACHES

TEACHING AND LEARNING COMMENTARY

Session one: shared reading

Ask the class to imagine that they are warriors who lived at the time of Beowulf. If necessary, give a very brief introduction about the lifestyle of such warriors. Ask them to imagine that they are sitting in a meeting in their Great Hall waiting to hear about a forthcoming expedition. Explain that all they will be required to do for this part of the role-play is to listen carefully to the details of the expedition.

Introducing teacher-in-role

NC En1 Drama: 4c
Drama activities: 11a

Explain that, on a given signal, you will be playing the part of a warrior called Beowulf, who will tell them about his expedition. If the pupils are not used to you working in role, make it clear that you will not be fully dressing up or putting on a different voice but warn them that you may use different kinds of words at times.

NB Less confident teachers may prefer to play the part of a messenger from Beowulf and read out a written message from him on a scroll.

The meeting convention is an efficient way to engage the pupils with the events of the story in a short space of time. The role-play helps the pupils to acquire a personal relationship with the text and creates a sense of immediacy and anticipation. The teacher-in-role is able to make these challenging texts more accessible to the pupils, by using language that the pupils will understand. The formal, elevated language used by the teacher in the role-play also serves to introduce the pupils to the style of language appropriate to a saga of this kind.

The role-play

NLS Y6 T3: S1

Give a clear signal to indicate the start of the role-play. Take on the role of Beowulf and tell the warriors your reasons for wanting to kill Grendel. Use a formal, elevated language register similar to the language used in a saga. Use a formal word order and vocabulary such as 'blood brothers', 'slaying the monster' and 'bravest deed'. Keep this section short and tightly focused and finish by talking about the need for you to select brave warriors for your expedition. Tell the warriors that you will return in a few days to hear about their bravest deeds, before deciding who will accompany you. Take off the cloak and announce the end of the role-play.

The request for evidence of bravery from the warriors is designed to create a purpose for written work within an imagined context. Hearing the formal, elevated language used by the teacher-in-role during the role-play will support the pupils in their attempts to write about their bravest deeds in the style of a saga.

Introducing the texts

NLS Y6 T3: T6, 10
NC En1 Group discussion and interaction: 10c

Show the pupils the covers of the three texts and ask the pupils which one they would choose to read in order to find out what happened when Beowulf went on his expedition. Ask them to give reasons for their opinions. Now show the pupils the copy or copies of the blurbs on the back covers and read them with the class in chorus. Conclude by asking the class if reading the blurb has reinforced their original thoughts about the texts or caused them to revise their opinions. Ask them to explain their answers.

The role-play seeks to motivate the pupils to consider and compare the three versions of *Beowulf*, in order to discover more about what happened. Pupils are thus encouraged to make some initial comparisons between the three versions during the first session, without having to read long extracts.

NC/NLS REFERENCES

NLS Y6 T3: T10
NC En3 Planning and
     drafting: 2a

NLS Y6 T3: T12, S1

NLS Y6 T3: T10
NC En3 Planning and
     drafting: 2b,c

ACTIVITIES AND APPROACHES

Independent work

Ask the pupils to start to invent their bravest deeds as warriors wanting to impress Beowulf. They should work in pairs to make an outline plan, perhaps using a writing frame such as the one below:

Plan for 'Our Bravest Deed'
Who went with you on your expedition?
Where did you carry out your bravest deed? Was it by the sea, in a lake, in a cave, on a mountain or moorland, in a swamp or somewhere else?
Give some details of what the place looked like.
What did you and your blood brother do that was so brave?
How did you feel about this as it was happening?
What did you do to celebrate your bravery?

Extension

Pupils could design an appropriate cover for a book about their deeds.

Session two: shared reading

You will need copies of three extracts from the texts, dealing with the approach of Grendel:

1 *Beowulf* by Charles Keeping and Kevin Crossley-Holland
   (page 17, from the start of the page up to ' ... within one minute he had swallowed the whole man, even his feet and hands')

2 *Beowulf Dragon Slayer* by Rosemary Sutcliff
   (pages 30–31, up to ' ... and drank the warm blood')

3 *Beowulf: a verse translation* by Michael Alexander
   (pages 73–4, from 'Walking to the hall came this warlike creature ...' up to ' ... even down to / his hands and feet.')

Outline of shared reading

Read all the texts to the class as they follow their copies. Talk about the appeal of each extract to a reader and point out the different styles. Divide the flip chart into three sections, one for each extract. Use the flip chart to record the pupils' opinions on the strengths and weaknesses of each extract.

Independent work

You will need the completed writing frames or notes from session one.

The pairs should now write the first draft of a summary of what happened to them when they carried out their bravest deed. Explain that they will be asked to read these out to Beowulf during a second role-play at the end of the week. Make it clear that the summary should only last about half a minute when

TEACHING AND LEARNING COMMENTARY

The writing frame is used to scaffold the writing process.

The role-play continues to motivate pupils to want to read more about the story from the texts and puts pressure on them to draft a concise, but exciting, summary of their planned story for the second role-play. Pupils are given ownership of the writing task by being asked to produce a synopsis of their own draft text.

NC/NLS REFERENCES

ACTIVITIES AND APPROACHES

read aloud. They should refer to their plan from the day before and use the extracts to help them make their summary as exciting as possible. Encourage them to use language similar to that used in the extracts. Pupils should write one draft copy of this per pair and then practise reading it aloud to each other.

Extension

The pairs should read their work aloud to another pair for constructive comments on what worked well and what could be improved or made clearer. Each pair should be encouraged to share the reading or read in chorus.

Session three: shared writing

Outline of shared writing

NLS Y6 T3: T10, S1	
NC En3 Composition: 1a,c	
Planning and drafting:	
2b,c,d	

Ask the class to imagine that they had all carried out a brave deed as a group of warriors on an expedition. Decide on what this will be and work together to write a summary of this to read out chorally to Beowulf during the role-play. This will be read out in addition to the pupils' own summaries.

Shared writing provides a model for pupils' own work and a finished summary as a safety net to use in the role-play, should pupils not complete many of their own.

Independent work

Ask each pair to carry on with their summary about their bravest deed. Leave the shared writing on display and encourage pupils to use this as a model to help them to use appropriate language.

Session four: shared reading

Outline for shared reading

You will need the shared writing on the flip chart from the day before.

NLS Y6 T3: T10, S1	
NC En3 Planning and drafting: 2f	
Standard English: 6a	
Breadth of study: 9c,	
11, 12	

Read the summary to the class. Ask them to think about how it could be improved and then how best to read it with expression in order to impress Beowulf. Discuss some ideas and invite individual pupils to give examples. Now read the summary as a group, incorporating the expressions agreed by the class.

The forthcoming role-play creates the need to ensure that the summary is read with appropriate expression in order to persuade.

Independent work

NC En2 Literature: 4i	
NLS Y6 T3: T10	

Ask pairs to finish their summaries and then decide on how they will share out the reading during the role-play. Then let pairs practise reading their summaries aloud.

Role-play provides a purpose for paired reading.

Extension

Pupils could write an adapted version of the class summary in the form of a book blurb.

NC/NLS REFERENCES

ACTIVITIES AND APPROACHES

TEACHING AND LEARNING COMMENTARY

Session five: shared reading

You will need:

- the shared summary on the flip chart
- the pupils' own summaries
- the cloak used to signify the role of Beowulf.

NLS Y6 T3: T10

NC En2 Literature: 4i

Outline activity

Arrange the pupils to stand in pairs in a semi-circle around the room or somewhere where they can easily read the flip chart and their own summaries.

Practise reading the class summary together and then give pairs a few minutes to practise reading their own work aloud.

When everyone is ready, put on the cloak to play the part of Beowulf and start the role-play or play the part of the messenger. Use formal language, as before. Turn to the flip chart and ask them to read out the account of the bravest deed they have ever completed together. Thank them for this account but tell them that you need to know more about how they perform when they are in danger with only one or two blood brothers. Invite pairs to tell you of their deeds and ask one question of each pair after they have read their summary. After each summary conclude by saying: 'You are indeed brave warriors and I shall be proud to accept you on my expedition' (or 'I think Beowulf will be proud to accept you'). Take off the cloak to conclude the role-play.

Role-play provides a context for the work and a sense of completion within the dramatic framework.

Sentence level

NLS Y6 T3: T10, S1

NC En3 Composition: 1a,b,c,d,e
       Planning and drafting:
       2a,b,c,d

Return to the three blurbs of the original texts and point out the differences between a summary and a blurb. Focus on the language conventions and grammatical features in the blurbs as examples of persuasive texts.

Independent work

Ask each pair to refer to the blurbs and compose a blurb for their own story, as if it were to be published in a book.

Plenary

NC En2 Literature: 8d

Read some of the blurbs and then point out the difference again between a blurb and a summary. Finish by reading pages 17, 18 and 21 from the Charles Keeping version of *Beowulf* about what happened when Beowulf finally fought with Grendel.

Unit 6
Using drama to support literacy

Through a variety of drama activities, pupils will explore the texts and develop speaking and listening, reading and writing skills that will support their literacy development.

Resources

Extracts from *The Iron Man* and *The Iron Woman* by Ted Hughes (Faber)

A shawl or scarf for the teacher to play the role of an elderly person.

A triangle and beater

Two scarves or cloaks to represent the Iron Man and the Iron Woman

Learning objectives

Two very popular Key Stage 2 texts, *The Iron Man* and *The Iron Woman*, are explored using a variety of drama activities. A number of follow-up activities through writing, reading and drama are also suggested.

Extracts from the units …

Explain that the drama starts as the farmers fill in the hole left by the Iron Man on top of the cliff. Ask the pupils if they will play the parts of the farmers in the story.

Ask the pupils to prepare for the drama by standing in a circle, as if they were the farmers standing around the hole.

Explain that, on a given signal, they should act as though they were the farmers, filling in the hole with imaginary shovels of earth from barrows or earth-moving equipment. Suggest that they will need to mime the actions but make it clear that, as farmers, they will need to speak to each other as they work. Ask for some suggestions on what the farmers might say, before allowing the drama to start.

Commentary:

Pupils are allocated roles as a whole group, requiring them to act and respond as if they were inside the story. These roles have been selected to enable pupils to operate as expert witnesses to the key events of the story. From these roles they will be expected to relate what happened, justify their actions as farmers and give advice based on assumed experience. Pupils now have the potential to talk about, respond to and write from perspectives within the text. This motivates speaking and listening and also helps to enrich the quality of pupils' written work.

37

(All NC references are for the programmes of study at KS2.)

NC/NLS REFERENCES

NLS   Y5 T1: T15
NC   En1 Speaking: 8a

NC   En1 Drama: 4a,c
       Drama activities: 11a

NC   En1 Drama: 4c

ACTIVITIES AND APPROACHES

Introduction prior to the drama lesson

Read the first few chapters of *The Iron Man* with the pupils. Read up to the point where the Iron Man is installed in the junkyard. Ask the pupils if they will take on the roles of the farmers at this point in the story. Explain that the drama will not be a re-enactment of the story in the book, but will be like an extra chapter about something that *might* have happened at this point.

Lesson one

Explain that the drama starts as the farmers fill in the hole left by the Iron Man on top of the cliff. Ask the pupils if they will play the parts of the farmers in the story.

Ask the pupils to prepare for the drama by standing in a circle, as if they were the farmers standing around the hole.

Explain that, on a given signal, they should act as though they were the farmers, filling in the hole with imaginary shovels of earth from barrows or earth-moving equipment. Suggest that they will need to mime the actions but make it clear that, as farmers, they will need to speak to each other as they work. Ask for some suggestions on what the farmers might say, before allowing the drama to start.

Use clear signals to start and stop the drama, such as saying the words 'Action' to start and 'Freeze' to stop. Make this a fairly short activity lasting only a few minutes.

Developing the drama

Introducing teacher-in-role

Tell the pupils that just as the farmers had finished their work, an elderly person came over the cliffs towards them, looking very distressed.

Explain that you will play the part of this elderly person when wearing the scarf.

Ask the pupils to sit down as if the farmers were having a rest and wait for you to appear.

On the word 'Action', put on the scarf to play the role and tell the following story:

You live in a nearby farming community by a river. Last year a factory was built by the river and since then the river has become polluted. Two

TEACHING AND LEARNING COMMENTARY

Whole group drama / mantle of the expert

Pupils are allocated roles as a whole group, requiring them to act and respond as if they were inside the story. These roles have been selected to enable pupils to operate as expert witnesses to the key events of the story. From these roles they will be expected to relate what happened, justify their actions as farmers and give advice based on assumed experience. Pupils now have the potential to talk about, respond to and write from perspectives within the text. This motivates speaking and listening and also helps to enrich the quality of pupils' written work.

Teacher-in-role

This strategy is an efficient way of engaging pupils' attention by engaging their emotions early on in the drama. The role offers a real-life stimulus that demands a response. It serves to set the scene and bring the focus of the drama to the forefront of pupils' minds. It also serves to set the tone of the drama by providing an example of how to work in role with sincerity and integrity. The teacher can also use this role to ask pupils to relate the events in the story from the perspective of particular characters, i.e. the farmers.

NC/NLS REFERENCES

ACTIVITIES AND APPROACHES

TEACHING AND LEARNING COMMENTARY

nights ago, you were in your bedroom overlooking the river, when you heard a terrible scream. It was coming from the river and when you looked out of your window you saw an iron woman screaming as she came out of the water. Once on the land, she stopped screaming and began to eat up all your farming machinery and other metal objects. This carried on until daylight when she went back into the river. The same thing happened the next night. Your neighbours are terrified and have left their homes. The police have been informed but they do not believe your story. You have heard about the Iron Man and wonder if the farmers can give you some advice based on their own experiences.

Pupils in role as experts
Staying in role, question the farmers about how they handled the Iron Man situation and ask them for their advice to help you solve the problem of the Iron Woman. Use the word 'Freeze' to stop the drama and then take off the scarf to come out of role.

NC   En1 Drama: 4a,c
           Drama activities: 11a

Reflection out of role
Out of role, discuss the advice the farmers gave the elderly person and ask the pupils why they think the Iron Woman was screaming in the water.

NC   En1 Group discussion and
           interaction: 3a,b,c,d

Follow-up written work to lesson one
Pupils can write a letter from the farmers to the elderly person's neighbours, describing the way the farmers solved the problem of the Iron Man. This can be in the form of a corporate letter written during shared writing, or individual letters written during independent time. If you intend to do this, it might be an idea to ask for the letter(s) when you are in role as the elderly person during the drama. Ask for the letter(s) to be left at the site of the hole in a few days time.

NLS   Y3 T3: T1
NC   En3 Composition: 1
           Planning and drafting: 2
           Punctuation: 3
           Standard English: 6a
           Breadth of study: 9b

During shared writing, identify at least two alternative courses of action that could be taken to tackle the problem of the Iron Woman. Refer to the way Ted Hughes chose to let his characters solve the Iron Man problem and encourage the pupils to evaluate this solution. During independent work, invite pupils to select the course of action they feel would work best and ask them to give reasons for their choice.

NLS   Y4 T3: T8
NC   En3 Breadth of study: 9d, 10

Use shared writing or independent time to ask pupils to write a new scene into the Iron Man story, reflecting what has happened in the drama so far. Encourage pupils to refer to the text they have read in order to keep their writing consistent with the style and layout of the original story.

NLS   Y5 T1: T15
NC   En3 Composition: 1a,d
           Breadth of study: 9a

Drama provides a context and purpose for a range of writing activities.

NC/NLS REFERENCES

NC   En1 Punctuation: 3a,b,c,d

NC   En1 Drama: 4a,b,c
           Dramatic activities:
           11a,b

NLS   Y3 T3: T1, 8
      Y4 T3: T9
NC   En2 Understanding texts:
           2c,d

NLS   Y5 T1: T19, 20
NC   En1 Drama: 4b
           Dramatic activities: 11b

NLS   Y5 T1: T15
NC   En3 Composition: 1d
           Planning and drafting: 2
           Punctuation: 3
           Breadth of study: 12

Cracking Drama © NATE Drama Committee 2000

ACTIVITIES AND APPROACHES

Lesson two

Story building

Working as a whole class, discuss and decide on one version of what might have happened when the farmers went to help the elderly person.

Whole group playmaking

Plan how to act out the chosen scenario in one of the following ways:

a   as a series of freeze-frames, where significant moments from the scenario can be depicted in a series of frozen moments or tableaux

b   as a whole class improvisation, such as the farmers luring the Iron Woman from the river with the sound of metal, in order to talk to her

c   as a play involving individual characters such as the elderly person or the Iron Man or the neighbours.

Whatever method is chosen, act out the sequence of events in sections to allow for reflection and possible re-runs.

Use the triangle and the scarves as props. The triangle can be used if the sound of metal is required to lure the Iron Woman out of the river or towards a junkyard. The extra scarves can be used to signify other characters such as the Iron Man or the Iron Woman.

Follow-up literacy work for lesson two

Mention that Ted Hughes has written a book about an iron woman, but this has a slightly different story line to the one in the drama. Compare and contrast the opening lines of the two stories and compare more aspects according to the needs of the class.

In shared writing or in pairs during independent work, ask pupils to write a playscript of part or all of the drama in lesson two. This could be continued in extended writing, if appropriate. One or two groups of pupils should be given time to prepare to act out the class play or act out their own or other pupils' playscripts so that the class has the opportunity to evaluate the script and performance as stated in objective 20.

Some pupils may like to write their own version of what happened to the Iron Woman, as if it were an additional chapter in the story of the Iron Man.

TEACHING AND LEARNING COMMENTARY

This gives pupils some ownership over the content of the work they will subsequently act out. Inventing stories verbally also helps pupils develop the compositional skills necessary for writing stories.

The choice of method here will depend on the confidence and experience of the teacher and the collaborative ability of the class.

a   Freeze-frames offer a controlled depiction of a story. The class can be sent away to produce the freeze-frames in groups, or the whole class can direct a group at the front.

b   Whole group improvisation offers complete involvement by the whole group but relies on the skill of the teacher in translating suggestions into activities suited to the whole class.

c   Making a play offers pupils the opportunity to struggle with how to present events in this form and provides valuable experience when pupils come to write plays themselves. This can be carried out in groups, or as a whole class directing one group. However, pupils with poor social skills often struggle to produce plays in groups and whole class directing can be problematic with pupils who have poor concentration spans.

Unit 7
Drama and narrative poetry: active approaches to pre-twentieth century literature

An exploration of the poem 'The Highwayman' using the format of the National Literacy Strategy. This can be used in Year 5, Term 2 (narrative poetry) or in Year 6, Term 2 (poetic forms), depending on the pupils' previous experience and maturity. It is a very popular choice of verse and this planned week helps pupils access pre-twentieth century poetry.

Resources

Copies of the poem 'The Highwayman' by Alfred Noyes

Poem-referenced character sheets, e.g. The Ostler, Bess

Sugar paper, felt pens

Photocopies of storyboard sheets

Glue sticks

Learning objectives

Through a variety of drama activities pupils develop their understanding of narrative poetry. They explore the richness of the language and analyse the motivation of the characters.

Extracts from the units ...

Divide the pupils into groups of four. Ask the groups to make a list, writing as 'King George's Men', of the crimes the dead man was suspected of. As you circulate, suggest that pupils focus on the word 'lace' from the tableau. Does this word place the story in a particular time? Direct the pupils to begin the crimes list with the phrase 'There is reason to suspect ...'. Ask each group to record the list on sugar paper.

Commentary:
The pupils are putting themselves into role as judges of the action, distancing themselves to write objectively yet with some knowledge of the man and the deeds that led to his demise. The teacher can help pupils access the setting of the poem by asking specific questions.

(All NC references relate to the programmes of study at Key Stage 2.)

42

NC/NLS REFERENCES

ACTIVITIES AND APPROACHES

TEACHING AND LEARNING COMMENTARY

NLS Y5 T2: T5
      Y6 T2: T5

NC   EN1 Listening: 2b, e

         Group discussion and
         interaction: 3a,b,c

         Drama: 4a,c

       EN2 Understanding texts:
         2b,c,d

         Breadth of study: 8d

Lesson one
Shared reading

Ask pupils to represent figures in the poem. They will make a tableau showing the lines 'and he lay like a dog on the highway with a bunch of lace at his throat.' Put this in writing as a 'title'. Do not read the whole poem to the class; they will do that later in the week. You will need volunteers to represent a highwayman and several of 'King George's Men'.

What can have happened here? Encourage pupils to make suggestions as to when, where, how, etc. Teacher input may elicit the following: he was a bad guy, the police were chasing him and shot him, he was running away from somebody. Take a role as the dead man's friend (who may also be one of 'King George's Men'). Pupils ask the teacher-in-role questions to find out more about the dead man's life. Let slip that the man (highwayman) had a girlfriend who had died in a tragic accident and that he would never run away from danger but was going after the men who killed her. He led a hard life ...

This is a good way of beginning by putting the pupils into roles that they will develop later.

NLS Y5 T2: S6b
NLS Y6 T2: S2b

NC   EN2 Literature: 4c
       EN3 Composition: 1a, b
         Planning and drafting:
         2a,f

         Breadth of study: 9b,10

Guided writing

Divide the pupils into groups of four. Ask the groups to make a list, writing as 'King George's Men', of the crimes the dead man was suspected of. As you circulate, suggest that pupils focus on the word 'lace' from the tableau. Does this word place the story in a particular time? Direct the pupils to begin the crimes list with the phrase 'There is reason to suspect ...'. Ask each group to record the list on sugar paper.

The pupils are putting themselves into role as judges of the action, distancing themselves to write objectively yet with some knowledge of the man and the deeds that led to his demise. The teacher can help pupils access the setting of the poem by asking specific questions.

NLS Y5 T2: T8
NLS Y6 T2: T5
NLS Y5 T2: S6b

NC   EN2 Understanding texts:
         2a,b

         Literature: 4a,c,f

       EN1 Drama: 4a,b,c

         Speaking: 1a,b,e,f

Lesson two
(Some reordering of the hour is indicated, but the 'balance' remains.)

Shared reading

Hand out 'character slips' providing information from the poem about characters to groups of pupils:

- The Highwayman
- Bess
- The Ostler
- Landlord
- King George's Men.

NC/NLS REFERENCES

ACTIVITIES AND APPROACHES

TEACHING AND LEARNING COMMENTARY

Guided reading/writing

The pupils interpret the characters from the character slips. Encourage depth of study and 'reading between the lines'. The pupils arrange to have themselves hot-seated by the other groups, working either in role or as themselves. If possible, questions should be in the form: 'If you …' (teacher highlighting complex sentence structures):

Encourage pupils to read slips aloud in pairs or groups, asking questions about unknown vocabulary or putting forward ideas about characters.

e.g. **Q** 'If you could escape what would you do?'

A 'If I could escape then I would take Bess away with me.'

NLS Y6 T2: S5a

The questions can be written up on an OHP/whiteboard for pupils to use as a model.

Pupils should record replies during this hot-seating session.

Word level work

NC EN2 Reading strategies:
1a,b
Literature: 4a

Pupils underline any rhymes from the text during the shared reading work and then find three more rhyming words to match each rhyme found, e.g. hair/there/where/care/share.

It may be useful to tape this session so that replaying it will help recall later in the week.

NLS Y5 T2: W6
NLS Y6 T2: W5

Plenary

NC EN1 Listening 2c,e
Drama: 4d
Breadth of study: 9b, 11b,c

In their original character groups, pupils interpret their character as a statue, one modelling and the rest of the group describing it to the class using words from the poem as captions.

This provides an opportunity for the teacher to elicit responses from other groups about a performance.

EN2 Reading strategies:
1a,b,d
Reading for information: 3a,c
Literature: 4a,c,d

Lesson three

There are seventeen verses but the last two almost repeat the first two. Save the purpose of the repetition for later (i.e. time lapse Y6 T2: T1b).

Shared reading

NLS Y6 T2: T9
NLS Y6 T2: T5

Give out the fifteen verses around the class (so in a class of thirty, pair work is possible). Pupils should not work alone. How do the pairs / small groups 'see' the picture that the poet is trying to paint in the verse? What is the story being told? Pupils make a freeze-frame from the given verse/s to show to the rest of the class later in the lesson.

Pupils should be encouraged to read the verse/s to themselves before attempting the freeze-frame.

Word level work

Ask the pupils to underline any words not understood from their verse/s and to look them up in a dictionary or write them down on Post-it notes to follow up later with the teacher.

NC/NLS REFERENCES

ACTIVITIES AND APPROACHES

TEACHING AND LEARNING COMMENTARY

NLS Y5 T2: T4 (part)
NLS Y5 T2: T5 (part)
NLS Y6 T2: W5

Guided reading

Gather the pupils together to read the whole poem to them *without the last two verses*. As the relevant verse is read, pupils will show the freeze-frames they prepared earlier at the same time. Some background music is useful here. This activity works best if the freeze-frames can be arranged in chronological order within the classroom or area.

Pupils will see the whole story in physical form, leading up to the crucial plenary question.

NLS Y5 T2: T6 (part)

Plenary

Tell the class that there are two more verses, then read them. Ask: 'What sort of poem is this?' Discuss this question (avoid guessing games). Then tell the class it is a *narrative poem* – link this to work done on fiction earlier in the year.

A good question to ask might be: 'What sort of poem have you just seen in these freeze-frames?'.

NC EN1 Group discussion and
    interaction: 3a,b,c,f
    EN2 Reading strategies: 1d
    Literature: 4c,d,e,f

Lesson four
Shared reading

Take all the sugar paper 'crimes lists' from lesson one and remind pupils about the first tableau they made. (Repeat the activity with the original 'cast' – they will remember what they did and who did it!) How do the crimes fit? Discuss thoughts from the group. Give each pupil a copy of the poem with numbered verses. The class reads it together.

Encourage pupils to read aloud with the required 'tone' for such a poem.

NLS Y5 T2: T4 (part)
NLS Y6 T2: T9
NLS Y5 T2: T8
NLS Y6 T2: T5

Sentence level / Guided reading

Ask the pupils to suggest the feelings of characters at various stages of the poem. They can record their suggestions in three columns:

Bess	Highwayman	King George's Men
confident	courageous	watchful

Remind pupils that they do not have to use words from the poem but if they do they should write them in quotation marks. This will encourage a good link into KS3 and level 4 onwards.

NC EN3 Composition: 1a,b,e
NLS Y5 T2: S6b
NLS Y6 T2: W5

Act as scribe for the class to show an example of the above structure and elicit responses for the first verse. The pupils repeat the above process with verses 3, 6, 11, 15 and 17, working in small groups concentrating on one character. (Split the class into three working 'areas', each one focusing on a single character.) Encourage pupils to find adjectives to encapsulate feelings – a thesaurus and dictionary will be helpful.

Plenary

Each 'area' feeds back the list of emotions at various stages of the poem. Make a master list of contributions for permanent class display.

The master list can be referred to as 'work in progress' and will be useful for the following day's activities.

NC/NLS REFERENCES

NC EN3 Composition: 1a,c,d,e
     Planning and drafting:
     2a,b,c,d,e,f

     Handwriting: 5b

     Breadth of study: 9a

NLS Y5 T2: T12

NLS Y5 T2: T13

NLS Y6 T2: T11

NLS Y6 T2: T12

ACTIVITIES AND APPROACHES

Lesson five
Shared writing

Introduce the idea of a 'storyboard' for the poem, which might be published in a young person's magazine. With the class (and this may take some time!), decide on the *nine* key events of the poem and the sequence they take, e.g.

- The Highwayman is seen galloping to the inn.
- He is talking to Bess while the ostler listens.
- He gallops away, promising to return.

Each picture should have a caption *from the text*. Remind pupils about the standard format for speech and thought bubbles, which may be in their own words (the 'crimes list' and the characters' feelings lists should inform this writing). Discuss the use of 'flashback' in the last two verses of the poem – how can this technique be represented in a storyboard? Who is telling the story?

Extension activities can include writing the storyboard from the point of view of one of the characters

TEACHING AND LEARNING COMMENTARY

Providing existing storyboard layouts may help, as may photocopied thought and speech bubbles for pupils to complete.

When all activities are complete, pupils may enjoy reading 'The Highwayman' illustrated by Charles Keeping. How does it compare with their own work?

Unit 8

Drama and a traditional fairy story: Exploring social and moral questions

The traditional fairy story 'The Emperor's New Clothes' is explored through a variety of drama activities. By the end of the unit pupils will have questioned the moral and social implications of integrity.

Resources

Story text

Vocabulary prompts

Items for context and role (hats, crown, throne, cloak, scroll, etc.)

Card, sugar paper, pens, pencils, etc.

Learning objectives

Through a range of drama conventions and the opportunity to work in a variety of roles, pupils will develop their use of different language registers and learn new vocabulary. They will develop their writing for a variety of purposes and for different audiences while at the same time exploring moral and social issues.

Extracts from the units …

In role as the King, walk around the exhibition, deliberately leaving the tailor's until last. You can praise and/or comment as you pass each exhibit. When you come to the last there is a dramatic pause, then you become effusive with how wonderful the costume designs are. You turn to your subjects for their responses!

Commentary:
Here the dynamic of 'revelation' should have been at work and the pupils will have been experiencing all kinds of feelings, particularly if you have played the King for 'real'. You may find that there will be a variety of responses!

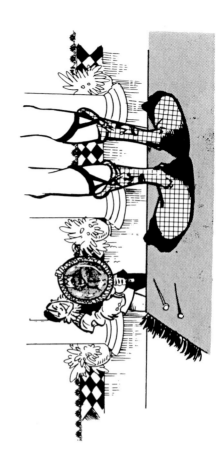

NC/NLS REFERENCES	ACTIVITIES AND APPROACHES	TEACHING AND LEARNING COMMENTARY
NC En1 Listening: 9a	**1** Begin by offering to tell the pupils a story – a very strange story of a King who had a serious problem: *Once upon a time, in a far off land, there lived a King and Queen. All their subjects loved them and were loyal to them. The King and Queen for their part loved all their subjects. Whenever the King and Queen were met, they were treated most royally.* Pause in the narrative.	**1** Pupils listen to the first part of the story 'The Emperor's New Clothes'.
NC En1 Listening: 2a En1 Group discussion and interaction: 3a,b,c	**2** The concept of royalty and status is interrogated. How would such royalty be recognised/treated? By judicious prompting, encourage pupils to contribute ideas.	**2** Allow pupils to demonstrate these in their own space, exposing them to: • use of space – staging! • use of body – movement! • use of voice – vocabulary, tone, volume, expression, etc.
NC En1 Group discussion and interaction: 10a En3 Composition: 1b	**3** Any new vocabulary generated can be 'boarded' for the benefit of the pupils and for use throughout the theme.	**3** Pupils may wish to record their work, e.g.: • A King and Queen should look … • A King and Queen should sit … • A King and Queen should move … • A King and Queen should speak …
NC En1 Drama activities: 11a	**4** Here you can use the opportunity to encourage groups to produce their own tableau/picture/freeze-frame, which they feel illustrates Kingship! Should you feel the pupils need more teacher support here you can have ready a list of appropriate titles for the tableaux, e.g. • 'The King knights a loyal subject' • 'A trouble-maker is banished by the King' • 'The Queen is presented with a gift'.	**4** Pupils negotiate groups of three to five.
NC En1 Speaking: 1a Drama: 4c Drama activities: 11c	**5** Ask pupils to share their tableaux and elicit responses from the other pupils as onlookers as to what they see as contributing to their reading of Kingship/royalty from the visual text. *NB* You need to ensure that the pupils merely read the visual text for clues that help them understand the message. You need to avoid at all costs this exercise becoming an opportunity for adverse criticism of any group's contribution.	**5** Pupils interpret the visual clues, repeating and reinforcing the concept of Kingship.

Cracking Drama © NATE Drama Committee 2000

NC/NLS REFERENCES

NC   En1 Speaking: 1a,c,e; 8a
      En3 Composition: 1a,b,c
           Breadth of study: 12

NC   En1 Speaking: 1b,e
           Drama: 4a
           Drama activities: 11a
      En3 Breadth of study: 9a; 12

NC   En1 Speaking: 1b,e
           Drama: 4a
           Drama activities: 11a

ACTIVITIES AND APPROACHES

6 Start the narrative again and continue:

But the King had one weakness, and everyone knew his weakness – he was terribly insecure, he lacked confidence, he just didn't believe in himself. When he had been a Prince it had been the same – he had to be made to feel important, even though he was important. He had to be told he was liked and admired even though his wife, the Princess, assured him all the time that his subjects loved him. She even managed to get the help of all their subjects so that whenever they met the Prince they would be ready to pay him a Royal Compliment.

You can stop and seek reassurance from the pupils of their understanding of a 'Royal Compliment'. You can provide examples. Ask pupils to write out their compliment. They could then read it out aloud. Responses should begin to reflect the elevated language appropriate to a subject speaking to their ruler. More confident pupils may, of course, be able to offer spoken examples spontaneously.

7 Finish the narration:

Well that was all right while he was just a Prince, but when he was about to become King, his wife the future Queen realised something more was needed. She came up with the clever idea of adding to the 'Royal Oath of Allegiance'. You see, she knew of the tradition of each subject making a personal promise to their royal sovereign at the coronation ceremony, so she arranged for every subject to add a morale-boosting ending to their speech: '... and I will always agree with his Royal Majesty and never make him feel a fool'.

Stop. You will now need to negotiate the 'drama contract' whereby pupils agree to adopt the 'as if' situation (they agree to pretend) in order to re-create the King's coronation and Oath of Allegiance.

You are setting up a situation conducive to eliciting a positive response from the pupils regarding their commitment to exploring the narrative through drama.

Agreeing the contract may appear simple and perfunctory but it establishes the prerequisite of any meaningful drama work – commitment and pupil investment in, and ownership of, the work they will create.

8 You can then enable pupils to organise and present the actual swearing-in ceremony. Pertinent and leading questions can guide the pupils in their use of space, roles and minimum props, costumes, etc. It will help to have some of these items to hand to lend some support to their creative endeavours; try to keep items to a minimum so as to avoid them becoming 'more important' than the drama they are making.

TEACHING AND LEARNING COMMENTARY

6 Pupils listen to teacher example(s) before attempting their own. Hearing the compliment spoken will encourage them to extend their language register.

7 Each pupil should prepare an Oath of Allegiance, being mindful of the Queen's command to finish all oaths with the same words. Formatting a style of elevated language response will contribute an essentially serious tone to the ensuing ritual/ceremony of 'swearing in'.

8 Pupils learn to acquire and develop an almost implicit self-discipline, working as they are within the structure of the accepted world of drama-making. The momentum and experience of the drama encourages them to accept the teacher as a facilitator and guide rather than as the expert with all the answers.

Cracking Drama © NATE Drama Committee 2000

NC/NLS REFERENCES

ACTIVITIES AND APPROACHES

TEACHING AND LEARNING COMMENTARY

NC En1 Drama: 4a,b
Drama activities: 11a

9 Now you are ready to introduce the convention of teacher-/pupil-in-role to further explore the theme. You will need to introduce the twin concepts of teacher-in-role as well as pupil-in-role. You will need to play the Royal Chancellor – the King and Queen's important servant. Using a hat here will aid identity and acceptance. The pupils will be playing loyal subjects of their King and Queen.

9 Pupils accept their roles as loyal servants of the King and Queen while at the same time reinforcing a reaffirmation of their commitment to the drama.

NC En1 Drama: 4a,b
Drama activities: 11a

10 You are now ready as the Royal Chancellor to welcome all the trades people/ artisans to the palace – trades people who have arrived by special invitation from the King and Queen. You infer they are excited that they might have been lucky enough to have been granted a Royal Commission – *for the King has decided that everything needs to be new.*

10 Pupils adopt roles as the loyal citizens and react to the teacher's exposition of events accordingly. They discuss the exciting news.

NC En1 Drama: 4a,b
Drama activities: 11a

11 As the Chancellor you tender all the commissions save one. How you allocate the commissions will depend on how well you know your pupils. The constraint device to use here that will still allow the pupils some ownership while at the same time allowing the teacher to maintain control over the 'learning curve' is to 'tender' the ideas/roles with inference, e.g. 'Ah! We have here a commission for designing a new royal palace. Is the Architect's Guild represented here today?'

You might have already pre-allocated all the roles – to ensure some degree of cohesive working relationships. Or you might await the pupils' responses and increase or prune numbers (always by judicious reasoning) to suit the dynamics of the class.

11 Pupils accept the roles offered, e.g.

- the Royal Architects
- the Royal Jewellers
- the Royal Household Items
- the Royal Carriage Makers
- the Royal Clock Makers.

NC En1 Drama: 4a,b
Drama activities: 11a

En3 Composition: 1a,e
Breadth of study: 12

12 Indicate that the Royal Family eagerly await their ideas for new designs and encourage the pupils to finalise them for Royal approval.

The one royal commission you have not tendered is that of the Royal Tailor, 'Mr Con Shark', whom you indicate has yet to arrive. However, he has sent a note saying he has been delayed. You express some concern/irritation but, nevertheless, indicate that work must proceed.

NB It is crucial, of course, that the issue of the Royal Tailor's commission is kept deliberately low key, as much of the future developing drama will depend on its successful revelation.

12 Pupils use the time allocated to prepare their original design briefs.

NC En1 Speaking: 1a,b,e
Drama: 4a,b
Drama activities: 11a

En3 Composition: 1a
Breadth of study: 12

13 Judging the pupils to have finished, you now (as the Royal Chancellor) invite all the trades people/artisans to the Old Palace where their designs can be exhibited in the Great Hall to be seen by the King and Queen.

There is a danger of pupils spending too much time initially on their visual work. The clue is in the words 'design brief'. You need the pupils to understand that the King and Queen merely wish to see their ideas in draft form; final versions can be produced later, if and when they get the commission.

13 Pupils set up the Design Exhibition for viewing by the King and Queen (in the classroom or larger space if it is available and judged manageable by the teacher).

NC/NLS REFERENCES | ACTIVITIES AND APPROACHES | TEACHING AND LEARNING COMMENTARY

14 — NC — En1 Drama: 4a,b / Drama activities: 11a

14 As the pupils begin to display their designs you need to ensure that a space is made/left available for the Tailor's 'Robes and Costume Designs'.

14 The pupils need to be aware that the space has been reserved.

---

15 — NC — En1 Drama: 4a,b / Drama activities: 11a

15 You exit and return, carrying with you the rolled-up designs from the tailor, but you are now looking worried and concerned. You explain that the Queen has sent a message to you that the King is feeling particularly fragile today. His nerves are really poor and he is not feeling at all confident. She is hoping that the exhibition will do him a power of good. You seek reassurance from the artisans.

15 Appealing to the pupils in role will elicit their willingness to help their King and Queen.

---

16 — NC — En1 Speaking: 1e / Drama: 4a,b / Drama activities: 11a

16 Ask one person to read out their 'Oath of Allegiance'. Stress the importance of the last part that the Queen was so insistent upon.

16 One pupil reading her/his 'Oath' out loud will remind pupils of the promise they made as part of the story.

---

17 — NC — En1 Speaking: 1e / Drama: 4a,b / Drama activities: 11a

17 Ask if it is possible for everyone to read that part out loud together? If this is accomplished well, you can end gleefully by saying you are sure it will perk up the King, and the Queen will be so pleased and grateful.

17 This will help all pupils to feel confident in their roles. It also provides an excellent opportunity for them to speak out loud as a group, and confirm their commitment to the developing drama.

---

18 — NC — En1 Drama: 4a,b / Drama activities: 11a

18 Make as if to leave to fetch their Majesties. You remember 'Mr Con Shark' the Tailor's designs. Add them to the exhibition and exit

18 Pupils may not react immediately to the shock of the tailor's con.

---

19 — NC — En1 Listening: 2e / Group discussion and interaction: 3c,d / Drama: 4a,b / Drama activities: 11a

19 This is the dramatic moment of realisation that you have been working so hard to lead up to. Having withdrawn from the drama, your observation of the pupils, apart from providing a fascinating and rewarding experience, should indicate to you when it is appropriate to return and move the drama on.

19 You will need to allow time for the pupils to register their reactions and share their responses with their neighbours. Few or no responses will indicate that they need further help and support.

---

20 — NC — En1 Group discussion and interaction: 3a,b,c,d / Drama: 4a,b / Drama activities: 11a

20 When the right moment arrives you should return with the news that the King is on his way.

Should the 'design sheet' of Con Shark the Tailor have failed to stimulate sufficient responses from the pupils, then you can (in role as the Chancellor) provide an appropriate prompt:

Oh! Dear, dear! What's to be done? This is a catastrophe! What will the Queen say? Goodness me! Too late, too late! Here comes the King.

20 Pupils should now be able to respond appropriately and wish to offer all kinds of suggestions. Control of this is provided with the statement 'Here comes the King'.

---

21 — NC — En1 Drama: 4a,b / Drama activities: 11a

21 Now is the time for you to remove the hat signifying the Royal Chancellor and to place the crown on your head so as now to be accepted in role playing the King. (A scary moment! But if the groundwork on role-play has been done and the pupils are committed to the drama there should be no problem changing roles and moving the drama forward.)

21 Here the pupils experience a real test of their commitment to the drama and have reinforced the necessity for 'suspending disbelief'. They need to understand and accept the convention of role change or multi-role if their drama is to move on and develop meaningfully.

NC/NLS REFERENCES

ACTIVITIES AND APPROACHES

TEACHING AND LEARNING COMMENTARY

NC/NLS REFERENCES	ACTIVITIES AND APPROACHES	TEACHING AND LEARNING COMMENTARY
NC En1 Drama: 4a,b Drama activities: 11a	**22** In role as the King, walk around the exhibition, deliberately leaving the Tailor's until last. You can praise and/or comment as you pass each exhibit. When you come to the last there is a dramatic pause, then you become effusive with how wonderful the costume designs are. You turn to your subjects for their responses! However, this is life-rate drama at work, so you can never be certain what the response from pupils will be. Therefore we have *options*. Options steer you through the developing drama and allow you to move towards a satisfactory resolution of the theme. At this point it is necessary for you to bring the drama to a halt and for everyone to come out of role in order to begin to discuss the 'realities 'of what has been happening. Usually by this stage the pupils can slip in and out of role with ease. You will need to recognise those moments when everyone needs to go back into role and when it is simply necessary to discuss matters as a whole class.	**22** Here the dynamic of 'revelation' should have been at work and the pupils will have been experiencing all kinds of feelings, particularly if you have played the King for 'real'. You may find that there will be a variety of responses!
NC En1 Drama: 4a,b Drama activities: 11a	*Either 1* **23a** No response from pupils – in which case you might summon Con Shark the Tailor to your presence. *Or 2* **23b** Children are keen to precipitate self-revelation. You can prolong the pretence in order that the tension of complicity gives depth of experience to the drama, e.g. *'You mean you don't appreciate the design?' 'Don't you think the materials and colours are wonderful?'*	*Either 1* **23a** The pupils will have to freeze-frame and then come out of role. A pupil volunteer is needed to be Con Shark. There should by now be no shortage of volunteers. *Or 2* **23b** The teacher can judiciously pace pupil responses in order that they may come to the moment of revelation by the King.
NC En1 Drama: 4a,b,c Drama activities: 11a	**24a** Having organised a volunteer, you should then return to the last moment of drama as a freeze-frame, with the pupil as Con Shark outside the drama space waiting to enter. Press 'play' and the improvisation can begin … **24b** It might be necessary to carry on with the pretence for some time.	**24a** The pupil as Con Shark will respond according to his/her level of confidence. Others will also be drawn into the scene and wish to contribute in role. **24b** Within the drama the pupil responses will be genuine and the pretend experience will add a depth of quality to all subsequent related work.
NC En1 Group discussion and interaction: 3c,d Drama: 4a,b,c Drama activities: 11a	**25a** It is essential within this scenario that you then proceed to manipulate the medium in order to move the drama forward to the 'revelation' of subterfuge/cheating. **25b** At some stage you will need to look for opportunities to lead pupils towards the moral dilemma of condoned subterfuge, e.g. *'Are you suggesting the Tailor is lying?'*	**25a** The level of control lies with the King – the pupils should respond as subjects and discipline is not lost. **25b** Sensitive questions and comments as well as your reactions in role as King should elicit a growing understanding as to what the pupils have become involved in.

NC/NLS REFERENCES

NC   En1   Drama: 4a,b,c
         Drama activities: 11a

NC   En1   Drama: 4a,b,c
         Drama activities: 11a

NC   En1   Group discussion and
         interaction: 3a,b,c,d

NC   En1   Speaking: 1a
         Listening: 2a,b,c,e
         Group discussion and
         interaction: 3a,b,c,d

ACTIVITIES AND APPROACHES

26a It might be necessary to carry on with the pretence for some time, but at some stage you will need to look for opportunities to lead pupils towards the moral dilemma of condoned subterfuge, e.g. 'Are you suggesting the Tailor is lying?'. Once the Tailor's deceit has been revealed it will be up to you in role as the King to quickly indicate inclusive blame of all artisans. It is essential to keep the focus of the drama on their willing deception of the King.

26b The result of this will be for the King to lose his confidence and to leave their presence feeling very sad and depressed.

27a The result of this will be for you, as the King, to lose your confidence and to leave their presence feeling very sad and depressed. Can things be put right again?

27b This is the time for you to come out of role to return and lead the class towards a resolution of the predicament.

28 The discussion work that takes place out of role should be an ongoing evaluation process leading up to the pupils going back into role whenever necessary in order to move the drama on to the obligatory conclusion. It will be necessary for you to both guide and shape the discussion work though judicious prompting in order for the pupils to gain some control over their own learning.

29 Some pertinent points you need to be aware of:

- How did such a thing happen?
- What did they/we do to contribute to this?
- What was wrong with the/our Oath of Allegiance?
- What can be done to help the King?
- How can they/we help the King to regain his self-esteem?
- Do they/we need to ask to speak to the Queen again?

This is one of the moments when it would be a good idea to go back into role. You may need to role-play the Queen (simply use the crown), or a pupil may be able to take on this role, with your support as Royal Chancellor (wearing the hat).

TEACHING AND LEARNING COMMENTARY

26a/b Pupils should begin to realise the implications of their actions in role: they will begin to show signs of guilt, regret and shame and may even attempt to extradite themselves from the situation they find themselves in. Too late, however!

27a/b The artisans will be left with the consequences of their actions! Now working with the teacher, they will need to come out of role in order to think through and rationalise what can be done to put things right again.

28 Pupils should be encouraged to question the outcome of 'their actions', and through pair, small group and whole class discussion come to a better understanding of the human condition. Pupils will have the opportunity to refine their skills of stepping in and out of role.

29 Pupils exposed to such astute interrogation will:

- offer more meaningful suggestions as a result of the drama experience
- be more able to recognise their culpability
- want to redraft their 'Oaths of Allegiance'
- have numerous ideas to redress the wrong to the King
- wish to do drama work so as to accomplish the need for healing
- easily step back into role whenever necessary, recognising and accepting that they, as well as the teacher can take on roles other than just those of citizens.

Here they may make some of the following suggestions:

- written letters of apology/sympathy/advice
- amending the Oaths of Allegiance
- designing real royal robes
- set up a Council of Advisors
- quality-control vetting.

NC/NLS REFERENCES

NC   En3 Composition: 1a,b,c,d,e
      Breadth of study: 9b,c;
      11; 12

ACTIVITIES AND APPROACHES

30 A 'satisfactory' resolution to the problem can easily be accommodated by a formal occasion planned and organised by the pupils whereby the King (teacher-in-role) is seen to be 'cured' through an appropriate scenario that has been devised by the pupils.

TEACHING AND LEARNING COMMENTARY

30 Pupils in role enact a 'formal presentation' designed to 'cure' the King, such as a special court occasion to celebrate his birthday, when apologies/explanations/new and finished designs can be presented.

Unit 9
Working from a shared text: exploring Galileo's 'secrets' through the eyes of his young daughter

These lessons, based on the picture book with text *Five Secrets in a Box*, have been devised to show continuity and progression from KS2 to KS3. The lesson plans are based around a central character, the seventeenth-century astronomer Galileo, and a common theme, his relationship with the young people who mean most to him.

The lessons may be taught in sequence or individual sections may be employed at the discretion of the teacher. They have been devised for a class group of up to 30 pupils. Space: flexible classroom space or the hall, which will enable whole class or small group activity to take place, studio space if available.

Extracts from the units ...

Return to the image of Virginia in her father's study. Establish the image using the simple props and a pupil in role as Virginia. Add a box, or casket, to the scene.

Ask the pupils to watch as 'Virginia' looks around the room. It could be suggested in the narration that the action is now taking place on another day. 'Virginia' discovers the box.

Commentary:
The pupil taking the role of Virginia could be left to discover the box, or more support could be offered by the teacher narrating what happens so that she/he can work within the narration.

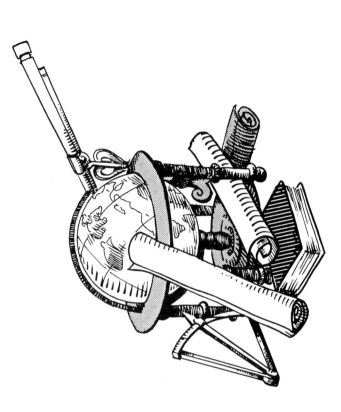

Resources

Overhead projector

White paper screen

Some simple props (i.e. chair, desk, some old books, feather pen, crucifix, cardboard tube taped onto a tripod to represent a telescope)

Copy of *Five Secrets in a Box* by Catherine Brighton (Methuen Children's Books)

Learning objectives

Engagement with the multiple use of drama techniques within this unit gradually leads the pupils through a sequence of fictional boundaries. Some of the boundaries are physical, such as the door to Galileo's study at home. Other boundaries are moral, such as the time to tell the truth or to hold back the truth. The text and images provide contexts for pupils, enabled by their teacher (sometimes working in role), to explore and enquire at the boundaries of established belief and perception. These parallel the enquiries of Virginia Galilei and her father Galileo, who must have experimented with such courage in a world jurisdicted by dogma and religious conservatism hundreds of years ago.

NC/NLS REFERENCES	ACTIVITIES AND APPROACHES	TEACHING AND LEARNING COMMENTARY
	The context	
	Ask the pupils to stand in a circle. A large ball is slowly rolled across the circle from one child to another, with the child rolling the ball calling out the name of the person they are rolling it to. When the pupils become familiar with this, another ball can be introduced using the same rules. Ask the pupils not to let the balls knock into each other. A third ball can be introduced, if appropriate.	Warming up activity.
		Check the fairness and pace of the activity.
		Children learn names.
	Stop the exercise. Then ask the pupils to 'rotate' the balls in the same direction slowly around the circle. Crouch in the middle of the circle while this is taking place and commentate on the motion of the balls:	Learning mathematical and scientific terminology in context.
	The balls are rotating around the circle. They are rotating in an anti-clockwise direction. The balls are like planets in their orbits.	
	Taking a ball yourself, ask one pupil to come and sit near you in the middle. Give her/him another ball. Tell her/him that s/he represents the planet Mercury. Tell the other pupils to watch as 'Mercury' rotates around you and explain that you represent the sun.	This activity promotes cooperation.
		This activity could be accompanied by music, e.g. from Holst's *The Planet Suite* (classical) or by William Orbit or Michael Nymen (modern). The music adds atmosphere but should be played softly – a reliable pupil could be asked to operate the tape/CD.
	Ask for another volunteer. This pupil is given another ball and told that she/he is the planet Venus. Both 'planets' are rotated in concentric circles around the 'Sun' in the centre.	You can control the pace of the relating planets from the centre and clearly offer the information.
NC En1 Listening: 2e, 9a NLS Y3 T1: T3	As the class circle watch, the teacher in the middle of the rotating planets slowly stands up giving an important commentary: 'Hundreds of years ago in the 1600s people believed that the "planets", instead of rotating round the sun, rotated around the Earth.' At this point slowly stop and guide the pupil representing the 'Earth' to the centre of the circle. Take up your new place slowly rotating the 'Earth', now at the centre of the circle. Stop the exercise momentarily.	You could indicate to the pupil operating the tape/CD to 'fade' the sound.
NLS Y5 T1: T5	Ask for a volunteer to take your place. Give her/him the 'Sun' ball. Explain that you are going to take the role of a character in the drama. The pupils should listen to what you say to find out more.	Indicate to the pupil controlling the tape/CD to fade in the music, softly.
NC En1 Drama: 4b	Start the rotation once more. Holding a scrolled document, walk towards the rotating 'model' and pretend to turn a handle as if controlling the model yourself. Speak the commentary as follows:	

NC/NLS REFERENCES

ACTIVITIES AND APPROACHES

TEACHING AND LEARNING COMMENTARY

My name is Galileo Galilei. I live here in Padua. I work in the university where I have my study. For years I have been conducting experiments to calculate temperature, mass and the behaviour of the planets. I have just left my house where I live with my young daughter, Virginia, and my housekeeper, Mrs Sarti. It is the 1st of October 1632. I am on my way to the university, where I have arranged to meet my students.

When you have finished, stop turning the handle indicating that the human 'orrery' (a moving model of the planets in rotation) should come to a standstill.

Pupils become the orrery. Indicate to the child controlling the tape/CD to fade the music.

NC	En1 Group discussion: 3a,b
NLS	Y3 T1: T17

Thank the volunteers and direct them to sit back in the circle. You are now out of the drama. Ask the pupils what they have just witnessed. Ask them to reflect briefly on the moment of drama they have just seen.

Strategy for reflection out of the drama. Use a role on the wall convention by writing the pupils' contributions on 'Post-its' and getting them to place these on an outline of Galileo drawn on a large sheet of paper.

NLS	Y3 T1: T9

Show the pupils the picture of Galileo's study (resource 9a). Ask the pupils to identify what is in the picture.

Set out the props you have collected, randomly on the floor.

Using artwork as visual stimulus. Use an overhead projector to enable the image to be shared with the whole class and referred to in the following exercise.

NC	En1 Drama: 4c
NLS	Y4 T1: T1
	Y5 T3: T2

Ask volunteers to place the props exactly as they see the objects they represent in the projected picture. This designated drama space in front of the picture is to become the 'set' in which the drama is to take place.

The pupils are creating a set in which the drama is to take place. They should be encouraged to make as accurate representation of the picture as possible given the props they have. This process should be allocated as much time as is necessary as the pupils are making an important investment in the context they are to work within.

NC	En1 Group discussion: 3a
NLS	Y3 T2: T3

Ask the pupils to identify what else they have found out about Galileo from a closer study of the picture.

NLS	Y4 T2: T2

Tell the pupils you are going to show them another picture of Galileo's study, which you want them to look at carefully.

This information could be added to the role on the wall.

NLS	Y5 T3: T3

Show them the second picture of Galileo's study (resource 9b) including the image of his daughter Virginia. Allow the pupils some time to look at this.

Here you are introducing more information in manageable layers.

NC	En1 Drama: 4a
NLS	Y5 T1: T5

Ask for a volunteer to be 'sculpted' as the girl. The pupils then 'sculpt' the volunteer into the picture.

Place the scrolls into the picture to complete it.

Select a volunteer who can control her/his position while being 'sculpted' by the other pupils. The pupils should carry out the sculpting one at a time.

NC	En1 Drama: 4c
NLS	Y3 T1: T3
	Y4 T1: T18

While the pupils look at the image they have created, read the first four pages of the book as narration.

My name is Virginia Galileo.

My father studies the skies at night.

Me, I sleep.

A new musical soundtrack is introduced. Classical guitar music is faded in slowly and softly.

NC/NLS REFERENCES

ACTIVITIES AND APPROACHES

TEACHING AND LEARNING COMMENTARY

*In the day he sleeps
behind a fine curtain.*

*Our house is quiet.
My silent slippers creep.*

My afternoon seems long.

*I rustle to his study
up wide stone stairs.*

*His desk is covered
with things.*

I look but I don't touch.

His papers. His instruments.

Stop the drama by closing the book and allowing 'Virginia' to come out of the drama and sit down.

Ask the pupils to reflect on what they have just witnessed. Ask them to suggest what the volunteer in role as Virginia might be doing while the narration is being spoken. Introduce the 'thought-tracking' convention to enable the class to speak out Virginia's thoughts.

You are offering the volunteer in role as Virginia support from the class to enable her to enact (mime) what until now has been a still image.

NLS   Y3 T3: T3

Tell the class you are going to run the drama again, but this time, Virginia's thoughts will be spoken out loud.

Tell the class you are going to run the drama a third time but this time Virginia can move in the ways suggested.

NC   En1 Listening: 2b

Taking the cue from the music and the narration, Virginia starts to move around the 'set' that has been created.

NLS   Y5 T1: T5

Stop the drama with the words:

*... I look but I don't touch.
His papers. His instruments.*

NLS   Y3 T3: T3

Ask the pupils what they think is written on Galileo's papers.

The responsibility for this simple piece of theatre is being passed from you, the teacher, to the class. At this stage some of the pupils may be in charge of the music and the narration. If the pupils are working in the context of a topic where there may be some previous knowledge relating to the planets, or instructions for using a telescope, or prayers that may be spoken when handling a rosary, then the scrolls may be blank. If you are providing information, the scrolls may have information written on them. For example, the scrolls may have a diary format on them, a list, sketches of the planets or a set of instructions.

NC   En3 Writing: 1a, 12
NC   En1 Drama: 4a
NLS   Y3 T1: T15, T4, T10

Now ask the pupils to work in pairs. They should create two copies of one of the documents.

There may be some negotiation regarding how the documents are going to be read by the pupils who created them (e.g. in what order, whether by a single voice or chorally) and what 'Virginia' does as she silently reads.

NC/NLS REFERENCES	ACTIVITIES AND APPROACHES	TEACHING AND LEARNING COMMENTARY
NLS Y3 T1: T4	After the appointed time (say ten minutes) has elapsed, they should place one copy of the document they have created in the 'set', retaining the other copy, so that they can read it out when 'Virginia' picks up that particular document in the drama.	
NC En1 Drama: 4b NLS Y4 T1: T5	Tell the class you are going to run the drama again with the music and the narration, but this time as 'Virginia' discovers the documents, they will hear what is written on them. Run the drama again with the volunteer acting in role as 'Virginia'. This time include your narration, the musical soundtrack and the pupils' spoken documents each time 'Virginia' picks one up to read.	Freeze-frame – marking the moment.
NC En1 Writing: 1b NLS Y3 T1: T9 Y4 T1: T2 Y3 T2: T8	Return to the role on the wall. Add the information that has been discovered as a result of the drama created.	The role on the wall is a reference point that may be used to end a practical session or to refocus the class at the start of a new one.
NC En1 Drama: 4b,c	Return to the image of Virginia in her father's study. Establish the image using the simple props and a pupil in role as Virginia. Add a box, or casket, to the scene. Ask the pupils to watch as 'Virginia' looks around the room. It could be suggested in the narration that the action is now taking place on another day. 'Virginia' discovers the box.	The pupil taking the role of Virginia could be left to discover the box, or more support could be offered by the teacher narrating what happens so that she/he can work within the narration.
NC En1 Listening: 2e NLS Y3 T1: T3	Re-run the drama. Narrate the next page of the book: *There is a box.* *I lift the lid. I peep inside.* *There are five things in the box.* Virginia takes items out of the box.	The teacher has placed a number of items in the box: a key, a necklace, a lens, a compass, some old coins, an 'extract' from 'The Starry Messenger' explaining Galileo's theories that the planets travel round the sun. This is important as it introduces the idea that Galileo had made an important discovery that was going to cause problems.
NC En1 Drama: 4c	The pupils can work in small groups. They should choose one of the items from the box per group. Ask each group to prepare a short 'flashback' that includes the moment when Galileo first acquired one of the items from the box.	Use the 'flashback' convention. This involves the enactment of a short scene representing a moment from the past. Give the group a time-scale and structure their work by referring to conventions they might use such as 'narration', 'marking the moment' or 'spoken thoughts'.
NLS Y6 T2: T11 Y4 T1: T6	After the appointed time, draw the whole class together and organise the sequence of the flashbacks cued by 'Virginia' lifting the individual item from the box and freezing while the flashback relevant to that object is enacted.	The sequence could be negotiated with the class, asking them to work out the chronology or rationale for the sequence.
NC En1 Drama: 4b,c NLS Y5 T1: T5	Enact the whole drama, building in the initial image, the narration, musical soundtrack, the spoken documents and the flashbacks.	This could form the basis of a class assembly or a performance for another class group.

Cracking Drama © NATE Drama Committee 2000

NC/NLS REFERENCES

ACTIVITIES AND APPROACHES

TEACHING AND LEARNING COMMENTARY

NC/NLS REFERENCES	ACTIVITIES AND APPROACHES	TEACHING AND LEARNING COMMENTARY
NC En1 Drama activities: 11 NLS Y5 T1: T20 Y3 T3: T5	Return to the image of Virginia in the room. Ask the class to choose a moment to freeze the drama as Virginia peers inside the box. While the class look at the frozen image, narrate a commentary which explains that '... Virginia was so engrossed in the box, that she didn't realise someone had come into the room'.	
NLS Y4 T3: T1	With a scrolled document in your hand quietly enter the acting space behind Virginia, in role as Galileo. Pause. Out of the drama, ask the children what Galileo is thinking.	You can indicate clearly to the pupils when you are in or out of role by holding or putting down the scrolled document. Employ the thought-tracking convention to discover Galileo's thoughts.
NC En1 Drama: 4c NLS Y5 T1: T5 NC En1 Speaking: 1b,c NLS Y4 T3: T16	Tell the children you are going to use a 'communal voice' conversation to find out what Galileo and his daughter said to each other. Once the groups representing Virginia's voice and Galileo's voice have been established, the dialogue between the two characters can be enacted.	Communal voice involves half the class sitting behind 'Virginia' and half the class behind 'Galileo' (teacher-in-role). Anyone representing Virginia (i.e. sitting behind her) can speak her words and anyone representing Galileo can speak his words. They should speak one at a time and listen to what is being said. Try to let this conversation run for a while even if there are silences. As the pupils acquire more confidence, the dialogue will flow.
NC En1 Drama: 4a	After a while, in role as Galileo and speaking your own words, tell 'Virginia' that you have a secret that you must share with her. Get her to promise that she will tell no one what you are about to tell her.	In role as Galileo, reclaim the dialogue using your own voice to introduce the new information. Virginia may be instructed to speak her own words at this point.

NC   En1 Listening: 9a
NLS   Y3 T3: T16
      Y4 T3: T16
      Y4 T3: T8
	Indicating that you wish to make sure no one is listening, read the letter you have on the scroll you are carrying.
	
	The Vatican
	Rome
	
	Galileo Galilei
	
	I am charged to tell you that the Court of Florence is no longer in the position to oppose the Holy Inquisition's wish to interrogate you in Rome, where you are to appear before the Holy Inquisition under papal direction.
	
	Cardinal Inquisitor on behalf of
	His Holiness Pope Urban VIII
		Forum theatre is a structured way of getting the class to direct the drama communally. As the dialogue progresses, any pupil can freeze the action by saying 'Freeze!' and then direct the actor to act or speak in a certain way. The pupil who is directing claps her/his hands to start the drama again. Individually or as a class, the pupils could compose a letter that is sent between father and daughter.

NC/NLS REFERENCES

NC   En1 Drama: 4b

NLS   Y3 T3: T16
      Y3 T3: T12
      Y4 T3: T23
      Y5 T3: T7

ACTIVITIES AND APPROACHES

Ask 'Virginia', 'Do you understand what this means'. Either continue to use the communal voice or employ forum theatre to develop this drama further.

In role as Galileo, gradually reveal your hopes and fears regarding the acceptance of your theory and the anxieties about the impending meeting with the representative of the Pope.

Explain that you may have to go away for a while and leave Virginia with the housekeeper, Mrs Sarti, but that you will write to Virginia regularly to let her know how you are.

TEACHING AND LEARNING COMMENTARY

Extension activity might involve the correspondence by letter between Virginia and her father. A useful resource might be *Galileo's Daughter* by Dava Sobel (Fourth Estate, 1999).

Cracking Drama © NATE Drama Committee 2000

Unit 10
Working from a scripted play: exploring Galileo's secrets through the eyes of his pupils

This sequence of lessons is based on extracts from Bertolt Brecht's Play, *The Life of Galileo*. Although the work focuses on the requirements of Year 8, teachers will be able to adapt it for other pupils in Key Stage 3. The lessons may be taught in sequence or on an individual session basis at the discretion of the teacher. They have been devised for a class group of up to thirty pupils.

The lessons employ drama structures as a means through which to investigate the text, the language of the text and the meanings derived from engagement with the text.

The tension during the drama stems from the internal dialogue taking place in the characters' heads – the human moral dilemma: 'At this moment do I say what I understand to be true or say something else, or remain silent?'

Resources

A copy of *The Life of Galileo* by Bertolt Brecht (ed. J. Willett and R. Manheim, Methuen, 1980)

Overhead projector, white paper and sugar paper

Audio tape playback unit

Some simple props (i.e. chair, table, cloth, some old books, quill pen, candle, crucifix, globe, cardboard tube taped onto a tripod to represent a telescope)

Extracts from the units ...

While still out of the drama ask the pupils to sit in rows as if in a lecture. Tell them you are going to assume the role of Galileo again. They will be in role as the pupils at the university. The drama will start towards the end of a lecture entitled 'The Starry Messenger'.

Now project onto the screen the text from Brecht's Life of Galileo (Act 1 Scene 1, pages 6–8: 'For two thousand years people have believed ... in chess too the rooks have begun sweeping far across the board.') Read the projected text. Ask for questions. Freeze the drama at this point and ask some of the pupils in role as Galileo's pupils to thought-track their feelings about what Galileo is saying.

Commentary:
Redefining the space.

Using a written script for shared reading.

Using thought-tracking for reflection.

Learning objectives

Engagement with the multiple use of drama techniques within this unit gradually leads the pupils through a sequence of fictional and reflective boundaries. Some of these boundaries are physical, such as the gateway to the seventeenth-century City of Padua or the university where Galileo teaches his students. Other boundaries are moral, such as the time to tell the truth or to hold back the truth in the face of the authorities represented by the Inquisition. The text, images and script extracts provide rich contexts for pupils, enabled by their teacher (sometimes working in role), to explore and enquire at the boundaries of established belief and perception. These enquiries parallel those of Galileo and his students in their courageous challenge to an establishment ruled by dogma and religious conservatism hundreds of years ago.

(All references refer to the programmes of study at KS 3/4.)

NC REFERENCES	ACTIVITIES AND APPROACHES	TEACHING AND LEARNING COMMENTARY
En1 Speaking: 1d	Sit the pupils down in front of the white paper screen. Project an OHT of the seventeenth-century map of Padua (see resource 10a). Ask them to identify what they notice about the map.	Project the map as large as you can for detail. The pupils might mention the narrow streets, the gate, the radiating plan of the buildings, the city wall, etc. Focus in by changing the position of the OHP or by cropping the picture with sheets of paper. If the work is part of a project, pupils may possess other background information. If not, they could be helped by some historical text (see Act 1 Scene 1, pages 6–8).
	Focus on one section of the map. Ask the pupils to suggest where people in the focused area of the city might be travelling to.	
En1 Speaking: 1d,e	Pupils work in pairs, identifying themselves as A and B. Ask the pupils to stand in the space in front of the screen. 'A' should imagine they live and work in the city and 'B' is a visitor to the city. 'B' with eyes closed, is led by 'A' around this part of the 'city' and shown the 'sights'. It is A's job to be B's 'eyes' and 'ears'. Practise 'freezing' the image of the people in the city. Freeze the image and tell the pupils the next time they freeze they will meet an important character who works at the university. Enact the 'guided tour' again. In role as Galileo (signified by a scroll in hand or a large old book), walk among the people.	The guided tour convention should be carefully controlled. A time limit should be set and the projected map should be left in place or copies of the map given to the pairs. After a few minutes the roles could be reversed
En3 Writing: 1g	Stop the drama by putting the scroll or book down and indicate that the pupils should sit down where they are. Project the image of Galileo's study on the white screen (see resource 9a on page 66). Ask the pupils to identify what they know about Galileo at this stage. Transcribe their ideas onto Post-its and place them on on the image of Galileo.	A device to indicate that you are out of role. Role on the wall. You can project the image onto a white paper screen and draw round the outline with a felt pen to give a permanent silhouette. (The pupils may be asked to write their own Post-its and to place them on the outline.)
En1 Drama: 4a		
	Tell the pupils you want them to create Galileo's study. Place the props listed randomly in front of them. Ask them to place the props, one at a time, as accurately as possible to represent the objects in the picture.	Creating the set, building the context. Props: table, chair, cloth, candle, quill, old books, documents, crucifix, globe, telescope, etc.
En1 Drama: 4c	Once the room has been created, tell the pupils they are going watch you, in role as Galileo, enter the study. They should watch carefully to identify his mood and purpose.	
En1 Listening: 2c,d	Holding a cardboard tube or a letter, in role as Galileo, enter the room as if you are familiar with it. Slam the tube on the table exclaiming:	Scripted or improvised drama.
	Telescope! Telescope! Those thieves in the market call this a telescope. Fifty lire and you can't see a thing through it. Will they make money out of anything these days? I must alert my pupils to this.	
En3 Writing: 1g	Out of the drama use the role on the wall convention to review with the pupils what they have found out about Galileo.	Use role on the wall for reflection.

NC/NLS REFERENCES

NC/NLS REFERENCES	ACTIVITIES AND APPROACHES	TEACHING AND LEARNING COMMENTARY
En1 Drama: 4a	While still out of the drama ask the pupils to sit in rows as if in a lecture. Tell them you are going to assume the role of Galileo again. They will be in role as the pupils at the university. The drama will start towards the end of a lecture entitled 'The Starry Messenger'.	Redefining the space.
En2 Reading: 1c,d	Now project onto the screen the text from Brecht's *Life of Galileo* (Act 1 Scene 1, pages 6–8: 'For two thousand years people have believed … in chess too the rooks have begun sweeping far across the board.') Read the projected text. Ask for questions. Freeze the drama at this point and ask some of the pupils in role as Galileo's pupils to thought-track their feelings about what Galileo is saying.	Using a written script for shared reading. Using thought-tracking for reflection.
	At the end of the lecture hold up the cardboard tube representing the fake telescope. Tell the pupils to 'watch out for such fakes being sold on the streets of Padua by Charlatans'.	
En1 Drama activities: 11b	Divide the pupils into groups of four. Ask them to devise a short drama in which a street vendor and his assistant 'con' passers-by into buying a telescope. Incorporate moments from the vendor scenes as 'flashbacks' within a re-enactment of the scene at the end of the lecture.	Small group play-making
En1 Drama: 4a,b		Building theatre by layering of conventions.
	In role as Galileo, dismiss the class, identifying one as Andrea, and ask him to remain behind. Galileo leaves the room telling Andrea that he will be back shortly and not to touch anything.	
	Thought-track Andrea at this moment. Use the text from *The Life of Galileo* (Act 1 Scene 5, pages 48–9: 'All of a sudden Andrea is standing by the rope … *They use these to pass bread through the window to Galileo and the old woman.*'), to explore the relationship between Andrea and Galileo.	The pupils will need to investigate for themselves the relationship between the characters.
En1 Drama: 4a,b En2 Reading: 1c,d	Use forum theatre to direct the pupil in role as Andrea. Does he look around the room? Does he touch or read anything? Place a scroll containing the letter from the Vatican in the set. If Andrea is not directed by the group to look at the letter, guide his movements towards it through narration. The contents of the letter could be projected onto a screen for shared reading.	Forum theatre enables a situation to be enacted whilst others observe. The actor and the observers can freeze the action at any time and suggest ways in which the action may be adapted, e.g. to be more authentic. Although a certain degree of freedom will enable the class to have ownership of the situation, the teacher agenda will dictate the discovery of the letter and enable the drama to move on.
En1 Drama: 4a	In role as Galileo, return to the room. Use forum theatre to investigate the action and the dialogue at this moment. Convey that, while Andrea is a trusted pupil who must continue the work although you must leave the area for a while, he must tell no one about the letter.	Action narration may be used: each character pauses before each action and each spoken phrase in order to voice, *out of the drama*, the motive for the ensuing action or speech.
En1 Drama: 4b En1 Drama activities: 11a,b	Working in pairs, pupils improvise short conversations between Andrea and a fellow pupil. Groups of four then read the text from *The Life of Galileo* Act 1 Scene 5, pages 48–9, and use the script to establish answers to questions that	The script used to provide background historical information.

NC/NLS REFERENCES

En2 Reading: 1c,e

En1 Drama: 4a

ACTIVITIES AND APPROACHES

might be agreed and written up on the board before they start work. The script could form the basis of a small group improvisation.

Ask the pupils to read the text from Act 1 Scene 11 of *The Life of Galileo* (Laughton version, page 249: 'POPE: No! No! No! ... These shuffling feet are making me nervous.'). Through shared reading, lay the groundwork for the trial of Galileo.

Having established who will be represented at the trial, facilitate the class to set up the trial scene – 'The Holy Inquisition of Galileo Galilei'.

Reflection on the trial scene could be facilitated by an overheard conversation whispered between Andrea and fellow pupils inside the court or guardedly outside the courtroom.

TEACHING AND LEARNING COMMENTARY

Redefine the space. Employ ritual for aspects of the trial scene.

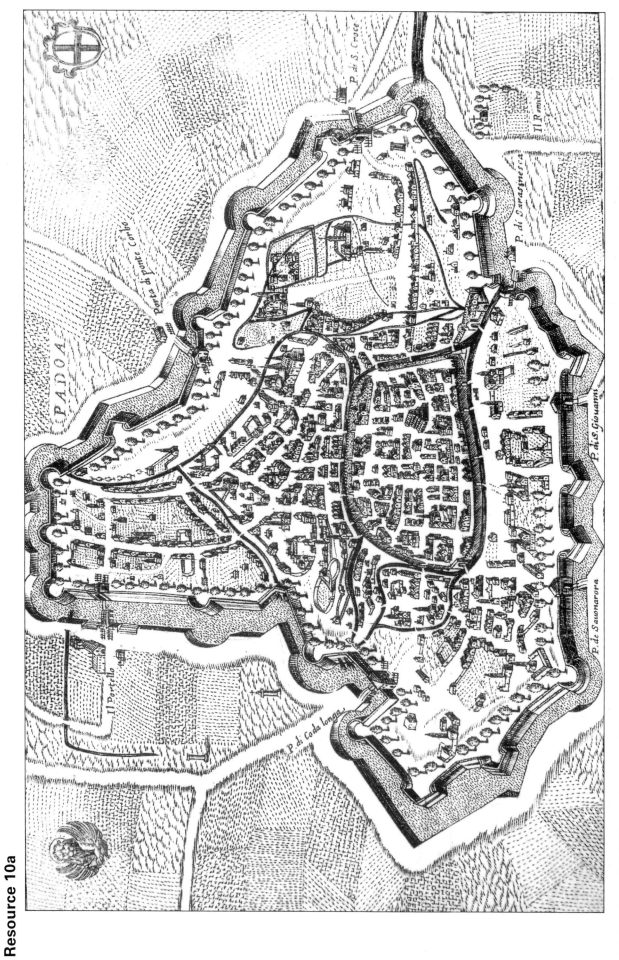

Unit 11
Conflict and resolution: using drama to explore the social, moral and historical context of a novel

This introduction to *The Iron Way* by Gillian Cross will address the issues of conflict and resolution. The novel is set in the heyday of the construction of railways in Britain at the end of the Industrial Revolution. Pupils will be introduced to a time of rapid social and personal change. Dramatic tension is centred on the physical wedge driven by the navvies through the countryside to build their railway and the emotional wedge driven between the villagers and Kate and Jem by their friendship with a special navigator, Conor O'Flynn.

Resources

Felt pens

Sugar paper

Post-it notes

A non-fiction text on the construction of early railways

Copies of the novel *The Iron Way* by Gillian Cross (OUP, 1979)

Learning objectives

Through drama approaches pupils will understand the build-up in tension in the structure of the novel and be able to analyse the text in more detail. In doing so, they will be able to develop empathy with the main characters.

Extracts from the units ...

Speaking now as narrator, tell the group that Kate accepts Conor as a lodger. Invite the group to form a 'corridor of conscience' for Conor to walk down; one side speaking as Kate/Jem/navvies and the other as the rest of the village, including the rector, Mrs Neville, the smith, etc. Ask a pupil to take the role of Conor and to report back on his feelings having been through the corridor.

Commentary:
This technique allows pupils to hear 'the other side'. Pupils should stay in their character groups.°

NC REFERENCES

En1 Speaking: 1a,b,c,g
Listening: 2a,b,c,d
Group discussion and interaction: 3b,e
Drama: 4a

En 3 Composition: 1i

En1 Listening: 2a,d
Drama: 4a
Breadth of study: 9a,c

En2 Understanding texts: 1c,d,k
Breadth of study: 8b

ACTIVITIES AND APPROACHES

Lesson one

Exploring the moral and social context: setting the scene for conflict

Establish a classroom arrangement that allows group work.

Explain that a natural area in the locality or a local playground is to be developed as a 'Park and Ride' scheme. (You could substitute a heliport/ supermarket/chemical plant – whichever fits your area). Ask the pupils to list the advantages and disadvantages for the area. The groups then feed back their ideas to the class. Act as scribe and draw together the groups' ideas, asking questions as you proceed: are there any 'parallel' ideas, e.g. people problems, money problems, construction problems?

Allocate the groups a responsibility as:

a   construction engineers
b   local adult residents
c   unemployed (builders)
d   board of directors of the construction company
e   local children
f   local bus company drivers/managers.

Ask the pupils to write down the four main points they would put forward at a public meeting to discuss the matter. They should be listed in large letters on a piece of sugar paper in order of importance. Circulate, encouraging discussion. Each group should choose a representative to speak. Pin up all the papers. Set up a public meeting to air the motion: 'This town wishes to have a Park and Ride [or other chosen facility]'.

Lesson two

Introducing an historical context

Pupils work in community groups as before. Ask them to read:

a   a non-fiction text about the construction of the railways
b   part of the first chapter of *The Iron Way* (from 'Grrrr-on!...' to '... peaceful valley').

Ask the pupils the following question, in order to put them into role:

As a navigator or navvy, what effect would you be having on the local area and its people? Think about the description of the navvy. When you write or say your comments, each one is to begin with 'I ...', e.g. 'I don't

TEACHING AND LEARNING COMMENTARY

If the teacher takes on a role as a local councillor here, it will support pupils' later attempts to take on roles.

Pupils learn that there are two sides to an argument and, here, can see the other one.

Matching the problems together into types will help pupils' writing further in this unit.

The teacher-in-role (as councillor) states that there will be a public meeting to discuss the problem. Representing each community group allows pupils to broaden their range of opinion.

Encourage debate and sincerity in the pupils' arguments. It will encourage empathy with the characters in the novel. If they follow up someone else's point and use it against them so much the better!

Having the same community groups as before helps cohesion.

Using an extract focuses attention on the newness of the railway. The teacher should draw parallels with lesson one. As pupils talk in role, they draw nearer to the novel's central character.

NC/NLS REFERENCES

En1   Speaking: 1a
      Listening: 2f
      Drama: 4a
En3   Composition: 1i,m,n

ACTIVITIES AND APPROACHES

care what I do for work as long as I can save enough for a place of my own.'

Give pupils five minutes to record their statements on Post-it notes. They should then read out the statements and post them on a display entitled 'A Navvy's thoughts and hopes' to refer to later.

In role as Jem, read the passage on pages 1–2 of *The Iron Way* (from 'He wriggled with excitement ...' to '... legs, wheels and earth.'). The pupils can hot-seat the teacher (in role) to find out what Jem's life is like. They may wish to make notes of your answers. Read the rest of the chapter together. To vary the activity, the pupils can read in role with a narrator.

Lesson three

Establishing a social/historical context

Using pupils as the main characters in the first chapter (not the navvy), ask them to establish a 'line of respect' for the villagers in the class. The characters should be:

    Rector   Mrs Day
    Jem   Ben
    Kate   Mary Ellen.
    Elisha Day

Note down the line in a reading journal or other record. The pupils then return to their desks. What criteria were used to establish this order? (Each pupil should try to give a reason why they should be where they are in the line). Ask: 'Where would a navvy fit in?' Link this question with their first lesson content. Say to the class: 'Ben's father is the blacksmith of the village. Put him in the line of respect.' Pupils in the line should contribute too!

Then ask the class to redefine the line in terms of *physical strength*. What do you notice? Pupils could make predictions about the path of the novel – use Post-its again. What will happen to: Jem? Kate? The navvies? The blacksmith? The pupils should give reasons for each prediction and find a phrase from the text to prove it, e.g. 'I think Jem will help build the railway because it says in the novel *"he stared, exhilarated towards the line. His thoughts were all of the future."'*

TEACHING AND LEARNING COMMENTARY

When the teacher models hot-seating this can lead to an increased confidence for pupils and deeper, more sincere questioning.

Through the 'line of respect' the characters are arranged according to how much respect they have in the community. Arranging characters in this way gives a sense of historical and social perspectives to the pupils. Use the pupils' reasons to comment on the male/female perspective of the time, the haves / have nots and, soon, the locals/strangers.

The more able pupils may want to do this text reference activity and teach it to the others later.

NC/NLS REFERENCES

En1 Speaking: 1c
     Listening: 2b,d
     Group discussion and
     interaction: 3a
     Drama: 4a,d
En2 Understanding texts: 1a,c,d,e
En3 Composition: 1d

En1 Speaking: 1c,e
     Listening: 2b,d
     Drama: 4a,b

En3 Composition: 1a,b,c,d

ACTIVITIES AND APPROACHES

Lesson four

The wedge – Conor arrives

Make a selection of examples of narration and conversation about different characters' points of view from the first two chapters of the novel. Ask the pupils to divide into groups and form character portraits of Jem/Kate/Joe H/ the navvies/Ben/Mrs Neville. After ten minutes, in role as Conor, approach each group to hold a conversation (all the other groups should listen). You may be asking Jem the way to Kate's house, or his navvy friends whether you are doing the right thing by leaving the camp to look for lodgings in the village, or announcing to Kate that you want to introduce yourself to the smith. I suggest you begin with the navvies group. The pupils record their opinions in a reading journal or other record.

Speaking now as narrator, tell the group that Kate accepts Conor as a lodger. Invite the group to form a 'corridor of conscience' for Conor to walk down; one side speaking as Kate/Jem/navvies and the other as the rest of the village, including the rector, Mrs Neville, the smith, etc. Ask a pupil to take the role of Conor and to report back on his feelings having been through the corridor.

Ask pupils to work in groups of three to create a freeze-frame of the effect Conor is having upon the characters in the story. If possible the freeze-frame should be a symbolic one. Pupils should try to make explicit where the characters' loyalties lie.

Lesson five

Conor

Assume the role of Conor again. The pupils hot-seat you, either as themselves or as one of the characters they were introduced to in the last lesson. If the questions seem difficult to tackle, step out of role and ask the group to discuss an answer for it. You may find that one or two of the pupils would like to take on the role of Conor, but make sure that the following points are put over in Conor's replies or comments: that he is a decent man and that all he wants to do is to settle down somewhere with a wife and some land earned by honest toil – he is tired of the nomadic life.

If a pupil does take on the role for this hot-seating, then offer support: 'Raise your hand if you get stuck and I'll speak on for you. Lower your hand when you feel comfortable to continue.'

Ask each group to write a diary entry as one of the characters from the novel about the meeting with Conor and their impressions of his character.

TEACHING AND LEARNING COMMENTARY

These 'condensed character' sheets need to be prepared before the lesson to avoid slowing down the approach. The teacher circulates, asking pupils to explain what they have discovered about the character/s. Listening to other groups gives a rounded view of the character.

If the teacher begins with the 'navvy' groups, it will re-establish what pupils already know.

This technique allows pupils to hear 'the other side'. Pupils should stay in their character groups.

The dilemma Kate and Jem are in should be evident. If the teacher can photograph these, it may create further interest.

The central character, Conor, needs thoughtful handling.

Pupils' independence should be encouraged.

NC/NLS REFERENCES

ACTIVITIES AND APPROACHES

TEACHING AND LEARNING COMMENTARY

Lesson six

Conflict in the village

En1   Drama: 4a,d

Speaking as narrator, tell the group that Conor eases himself into Kate and Jem's home and changes the atmosphere. He brings a thank-you gift of a large piece of salt beef and after the meal wishes to take a turn about the village to meet the village men.

Moving on the plot helps pupils' concentration. The teacher may ask about the predictions the pupils had made.

En2   Understanding texts: 1h

In groups of seven or eight, the pupils then improvise what happens when Conor walks into the forge. One pupil takes the role of Conor, one of Jem and one of the smith; the others are members of the village.

Impress upon the pupils that *no physical contact* must occur in the improvisation.

Lack of contact makes speaking and listening absolutely necessary. Stopping the action focuses the group's attention on the tension of conflict.

Be bold about stopping the action to ask 'What would happen if …?' and changing the pupils' views of the action. Tell the group that no fight occurs. The pupils then read with you the passage on page 50 of the novel (from '"Well now," he looked round at them all …' to 'it could be that they were.').

Ask the pupils to work in pairs as Jem and Conor returning home. Ask the pairs to improvise the continuing conversation and to work out what both Jem and Conor really want to say, but dare not

Insist on *realistic* conversations. This will make the drama more powerful.

e.g.   JEM: *You're a coward.*
        CONOR: *I could have been in trouble there.*

Ask them to say it across a small space or side-by-side at a desk so all the group hears all the potential conversations.

Discuss the conflict of interest between:

* Joe and Conor
* Jem and Conor.

Unit 12
'Faces behind the Masks': Drama and ICT

'Faces behind the masks' uses drama conventions to explore texts, issues and dilemmas. It demonstrates the use of CD-ROM, the internet, other computer programs and the media as an interactive resource for drama. Pupils are encouraged to question the ways in which individuals are often forgotten within historical events and think about the real lives that lie behind the news stories they see or read about.

Resources

When planning any project involving ICT and drama it is necessary to recognise that access to equipment, space and expertise varies from school to school. If the ideas and conventions are at the centre of the work, teachers can adapt their approach according to what is available.

The following would be found useful: a copy of *Rose Blanche* by Roberto Innocenti (Harcourt, Brace & Co., 1996), a picture map of an Eastern European city, relevant images, plain white masks, copy of the playscript *Bretevski Street*.

One computer, with access to the Internet, would be sufficient for many of the suggested activities.

Learning objectives

The use of ICT and drama, within this project, encourages pupils to recognise faces behind masks, individuals behind historical events and real lives behind news stories. Many successful ICT simulations have required pupils to 'wear' the masks and 'hide' behind a pretence, rather than acknowledge the fictional environment and, therefore, be able to explore the relationship between the imagined and the real.

By entering this imaginative and symbolic environment they can safely challenge, affirm and explore identities, relationships, values, cultures and contexts, in ways which strengthen their self-esteem. (NATE Drama Position Paper, 1998)

What this unit aims to achieve is that pupils not only find faces and lives, through information-retrieval skills, but both create and explore their own, so that the use of ICT is not just a factual resource but a creative and interactive medium.

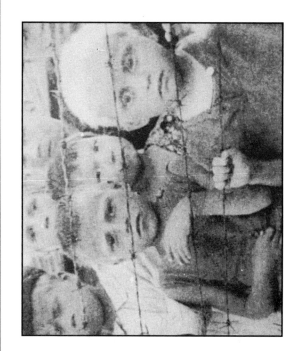

Extracts from the units ...

Ask the pupils to read extract C in pairs. Then, as a whole group, watch a pair. Stop the drama at 'MY POTATOES' and ask the pupils to think about what the characters would say or think next. When they have made suggestions ask them to stand behind the character for whom they have spoken. Once several pupils (or all the pupils) have made suggestions and have stood behind the appropriate characters, re-run the scene, this time hearing the communal voices.

Commentary:
Forum theatre can be used here to encourage pupils to think about the characters' reactions, intention, actions and ideas – through the suggestions that they make and the discussion that takes place.

NC/NLS REFERENCES	ACTIVITIES AND APPROACHES	TEACHING AND LEARNING COMMENTARY
	Children of the Holocaust **Rose Blanche**	
EN1 Drama: 4a,b,c,d Drama activities: 11a,c	*Rose Blanche* by Roberto Innocenti is an excellent resource/stimulus for drama, media education, history and ICT. The two pictures of the children behind the barbed wire provide a good starting point for drama. Ask the pupils, using themselves to re-create the picture and begin to discuss what they can read in the picture. Plain white masks can be worn at this stage to help create the sense of the unknown person – the face we don't want to recognise.	Read the story up to the page when Rose is about to see the children behind the barbed wire. Ask the pupils, using evidence from the text and pictures, to say what they think she sees.
	The picture can also be created in stages, showing small parts of it at a time (e.g. Rose kneeling down in the snow passing something to another child, then adding more children). Discussion can take place about the picture. How might the barbed wire be represented? A line of pupils can be positioned as the barbed wire and speak as if explaining its role, its history, what it sees. The picture can then be developed by questioning in role, speaking thoughts, Rose talking to the children, etc.	The aim is to re-create the sense of the children behind the wire. The masks are deliberate – as they hide the reality of the faces.
	Using the internet	
EN2 Printed and ICT-based information texts: 4a,b,c,d Non-fiction and non-literary texts: 9b	The photograph of the children behind the barbed wire at Auschwitz shown in resource 12a can be found on a number of web sites, e.g. http://www.euronet.nl/users/jubo/holocaust.html	
	You can use this picture instead of, or alongside, the *Rose Blanche* pictures. If a projector is available, the picture can be projected onto a wall once the pupils have established their own picture.	The speaking of the lines directly from the biographies begins the process of placing faces on the masks as well as raising some difficult issues about how masks are used to prevent us seeing the faces. This can then be developed further to produce a photograph album / series of pictures. If the pupils return to the same position with the masks but this time produce another scene from childhood, e.g. waiting, looking out for their parents to return from work, then the ideas are developed. The masks can be revealed and new lines spoken.
EN1 Drama: 4a,b,d	To reveal the faces behind the masks, photographs of the children, taken from the biographies on the web site http://www.wiesenthal.com/children/prvchild.htm can be used (again projected onto a screen if possible). The information in the biographies can then be used for more drama. Still pictures from the past can be created – a photograph album from the child's life (emphasising contrasts etc.). Characters can be repositioned according to the effect they have on different aspects of the child's life, the events of the Holocaust, etc. The space between characters can be described 'the space of ... *hatred, ignorance, fear...*' Scenes can be created.	

NC/NLS REFERENCES

EN1 Drama: 4a,d
Listening: 2c; 9c
Group discussion and interaction: 3a

EN1 Drama: 4a
EN2 Printed and ICT-based information texts: 4a
Non-fiction and non-literary texts: 9b
EN3 Breadth of study: 9b

ACTIVITIES AND APPROACHES

Masks

The idea of 'masks' provides a focus for discussing and exploring students' and others' understanding of the Holocaust. Questions can be raised such as: How were 'masks' used then and since then to cover up reality? How are terms like 'The Final Solution' and 'The Holocaust' themselves a way of masking the reality? Pupils can create pictures (on screen or using drama) to show the 'masks' that were used to hide reality.

Perpetrator, victim and bystander

During several of the above activities, particularly when still pictures are being used (recreating scenes from *Rose Blanche*), ask the pupils to place the perpetrator, bystander, victim in the picture. Then give the pupils a chance to move them according to their distance from certain characters, the events, how responsible they are for the events in the picture and the space between them and the characters described. Other people in role, or the pupils themselves (members of today's community), can then be placed in the picture in the same way. These three terms, and what they actually mean, are also a useful way of exploring more recent historical/news events.

Using e-mail

E-mail has tended to be used in schools purely as an alternative method of communication with a 'real' person and/or expert, so that pupils can enter into dialogue or request information. Within a drama context, however, it can also be used as another way of developing a role/character. Questioning in role on-line could be a useful way of developing the drama by providing visual images alongside text and using 'the mantle of the expert' in a new context. If resources allow, pupils could send messages to each other, and respond in role to develop the drama.

You could prepare and send some messages before the lesson, to be opened during it. This provides another way of placing a face on the mask (even if that face is fictional). For example, a message might be sent from a television producer who wants to create a programme about the children of the Holocaust. The pupils could respond on-line after they have researched the subject further and developed the drama.

(See http://www.spa3.k12.sc.us/WebQuests/Anne%20Frank/index.html)

TEACHING AND LEARNING COMMENTARY

By describing the space between the characters and physically positioning the others in the picture in relation to each other, pupils are asked to question, in some depth, the relationships and responsibilities. It allows them to see this visually and argue effectively why they want, for example, to move someone from an earlier position they have been placed in by another pupil. The same still picture, or another, can be used and given a descriptive sentence from an event in the current news. If the three terms (victim, perpetrator, bystander) are used again in this context, some very interesting discussions can take place.

There is a great deal of potential for using e-mail in drama. What is important is that the pupils and teacher are clear of the roles they are to develop and sustain. Questions do need to be raised as to its purpose in relation to such approaches as teacher in role. The ability to research an issue and respond in this way, however, allows the pupils to manipulate and organise words (both spoken and printed).

NC/NLS REFERENCES

ACTIVITIES AND APPROACHES

TEACHING AND LEARNING COMMENTARY

EN1 Drama: 4a
Speaking: 1a,c,d; 8a
Listening: 2a,f; 9a
Group discussion and
interaction: 3a

Stars

The shape of the star (which the Jewish children were made to wear) is another symbol/image that could be developed through drama. A large star should be placed on the floor (or imagined) and different images created at each point. The six points should show: the death camps, random killings, the ghetto, victim, perpetrator and bystander. The pupils should be asked to decide, for example, who needs to be nearest the centre of the star, which images should be nearest to each other, how they are linked by a line across the star.

The pupils standing in a star formation could take single lines from the biographies and speak them in turn. These could also include lines from the poem 'Daniel' (see below) and other sources. The pupils finally say their lines in a round in order to create a 'sound montage' of children's voices and memories. The same idea could be developed on screen, building up the shape of a star from images and text.

The shape of the star with its opposites (far apart yet linked) lends itself to drama and discussion, providing the pupils with a visual image to help explore the issues. By physically moving and questioning the distances, the pupils bring themselves into the issue, while remaining in a 'safe' position.

Poetry: ICT and/or drama?

EN1 Drama: 4a,b,d
Drama activities: 11a,b,c
Speaking 8a,b,c
Listening: 9a

EN2 Understanding texts:
1a,b,c,d,g,h

The poem 'Daniel' also appears on a number of web sites, e.g. http://www.mtsu.edu/~baustin/daniel.html

'Daniel' by Laura Forgette Crist
And the child held her hand
A child tiny for almost eight,
Deep blue eyes that dominated his face,
When he explained new events to her,
*   that funny doggy,*
*   that pretty rock,*
And the freckles on his cheek,
No one saw a sunrise more perfect,
*   to her,*
She so vividly smells the fragrance of
*   his hair,*
*   his ears,*
*   his breath in the morning*
She vividly hears that little heartbeat,
*   that was hers*
*   always hers,*
*   and the laughter,*
*   that raspy little laugh,*
when he caught her in a conundrum.
All this,
But this is merely the surface,
As she watches her little God sheared,
*   and stripped,*
For the gas chamber.

This poem, like the *Rose Blanche* text, lends itself to a variety of work in drama and ICT. The poem can be used in a number of different ways – presenting the scene when the story of Daniel is told, still pictures, past history, bringing the poem to life, images, etc. By having the poem on screen, your pupils can alter and add to the text, perhaps interrupting after every two lines with thoughts/ description, or pictures arrived at by questioning in role, the use of other drama conventions or research.

Following a similar process, pupils can interrupt the poem after every two lines with a piece of drama, using the line from the poem as the first line of their drama. This works extremely well with song lyrics if a tape is stopped and the pupils begin each piece of drama with the last line that was sung. Are there songs that could be used alongside the poem and/or this topic?

A wide range of teaching and learning opportunities exist here. By bringing the poem 'to life', or through other activities, pupils are asked to engage directly with the events and grasp an understanding of both the structure of the poem and the language used.

The 'interruption' of the poem with work in role encourages pupils to focus on the relationship between writer, reader and text and transfer this understanding to the wider subject or a current event / aspect of their lives. If these 'interruptions' are also made on screen, with images or the pupils' own writing, an interesting comparison could be made with the drama, enabling pupils to explore their reactions to the poems in greater depth.

Possibilities for media work, writing in role, the use of music and literary analysis also exist.

Cracking Drama © NATE Drama Committee 2000

Other web sites

One web site that is certainly worth looking at is:
http://www.spa3.k12.sc.us/WebQuests/Anne%20Frank/index.html

not only because of all the other Holocaust sites it refers to (particularly those providing access to pictures and photographs) but because the idea of pupils creating a documentary after visiting various web sites and making decisions about music, art, content, etc., could be a useful format to follow for a whole range of topics/issues. The web sites concerning the art and music created in the concentration camps might help teachers consider how music and art from the Holocaust could be used within the drama and ICT work.

EN2   Printed and ICT-based information texts: 4a,b,c,d

Non-fiction and non-literary texts: 9b

Using ICT, pupils are able to research an issue and can manipulate and organise words (spoken and written) for a specific purpose and a specific audience. For example, using PowerPoint pupils can prepare a presentation for younger children on the issue of prejudice or the Holocaust.

Current events and news coverage

The ideas explored in the above activities could be taken a step further by looking at a current news story (Middle East conflicts, Northern Ireland – see below), possibly on-line, and following through the idea of placing faces and lives within news stories/events to explore the idea that we don't really *see* individuals (people we recognise) and until we directly relate to events they don't have the same significance (bystanders or perpetrators?).

The use of masks and seeing the faces behind them can again be used to give faces to still pictures where masks have been used. It is useful, however, to bear in mind that ICT has a purpose beyond factual research and can be used for interaction / mantle of expert conventions, creative writing activities and the manipulation of images and words (spoken and written). Thinking about perpetrators, victims and bystanders in this context, placing them in the picture, and comparing them with the children of the Holocaust images / still pictures would create some very interesting work/ideas.

EN1   Drama: 4a,
EN2   Printed and ICT-based information texts: 4a,b,c,d

Non-fiction and non-literary texts: 9b

Many of the activities developed so far could be repeated to explore a current story or event. Repeating the activities, using a different issue or event, encourages the pupils to make links and consider the issue/idea within a 'safe' context.

Hate appearing in your life

A statement that frequently appears on the Holocaust sites – 'Hate appearing in your life' could be explored through the use of ICT and drama and provides a link between the Holocaust, current events and the pupils' own understanding/feelings. Images of childhood could, starting with this statement, be another focus for ICT and drama to explore the child's view of him/herself, how others see him/her and how others see childhood and his/her place in the wider community. Drama conventions could allow the pupils to question when 'hate' appeared in their lives (and that of others), what it has meant to them, how it has changed, etc. The sense of perpetrators, victims and bystanders could again be explored here.

EN1   Drama: 4a,b
EN2   Printed and ICT-based information texts: 4a,b,c,d

Non-fiction and non-literary texts: 9b

This could become a whole topic in itself. The extracts from 'As If' can, however, be used very successfully alongside the earlier images/poem. Interesting issues are raised about the media's manipulation of faces/masks that could provide the material for the media assignment within GCSE English (e.g. images of childhood: faces or masks?).

ACTIVITIES AND APPROACHES

And....

As explained on page 73, many of the above suggestions can serve only as brief outlines for possible approaches to using drama and ICT and can only cover a limited range of work in this area (without moving into the use of CD-ROMs and different types of software).

TEACHING AND LEARNING COMMENTARY

Although the focus has been on a particular topic, individual teachers will be able to adapt many of these approaches to cover another subject, topic or aspect of the curriculum.

The ideas and approaches suggested here should enable the teacher to consider using ICT and drama in her/his teaching and/or to create links with literary, non-literary and media texts.

Faces and masks in Kosovo and *Bretevski Street* by Lin Coghlan

This unit of work can be linked to the preceding one, to make the ideas and issues more immediate. It can also easily be developed as a unit in its own right.

Picture map of an Eastern European (or other) city

EN1 Speaking: 1a,b,c,d; 8a
Listening: 2a,f; 9a,c
Drama: 4a,b

EN2 Printed and ICT-based information texts: 4b,c

Using either a CD-ROM (a variety of 2D and 3D atlases versions are available) or other ICT facility, show the pupils the city map. If appropriate ICT facilities are not available, a suitable map can be copied onto an OHT. Organise the pupils to work in pairs, and set up a guided tour situation. For this activity, one of the pupils needs to imagine that he/she knows the place well and, using the picture/map, take his/her partner on a guided tour of the city, describing and commenting on some of the things that they can see around them. The other pupil keeps his/her eyes closed and allows him/herself to be guided around, listening to the description and asking appropriate questions if necessary.

As the pupils lead each other working from a projected map or picture, they not only explore in an imaginative way, the historical or geographical environment, but simultaneously explore the space of the classroom and their collaborative relationship.

After a few minutes, ask the pupils to explain what they were 'shown' as they made their way around the city. You might want to give specific prompts here by asking what sounds they heard or what smells they remember as well as asking them to describe specific aspects of the city in detail.

Bretevski Street – The Mother's Box

EN1 Drama: 4a,
Speaking: 1b,c,d; 8a
Listening: 2a; a,c

Place several items (relevant to the text – potato, crucifix, etc.) in a box and ask the pupils to work in pairs. The poem 'Daniel' (see page 76) could be one item in the box, particularly if the last two lines were missing (ripped from the page?). One of the pupils from each pair comes and collects one of the items from the box, without the other seeing it, while the other pupil is given a piece of paper and a pen/pencil. The pupils sit with their backs to each other. The pupil with the object describes the item to his/her partner while the other person has to draw what he/she thinks is being described. To develop the drama, someone can be chosen to sit with the box while the pupils, in silence, bring their objects back to the box, pass them to its owner and watch as he/she places them in the box. Ritual is introduced in this way, together with a very limited sense of role.

This is a good way of starting off a session as it gets students immediately involved and working together, as well as allowing for links with subsequent drama activities.

NC/NLS REFERENCES

EN1 Drama: 4a,b,c
     Drama activities: 11b,c
EN2 Understanding texts:
     1a,b,c,h,i

EN1 Drama: 4a,b,c
     Listening: 9a

EN1 Drama: 9a,
EN2 Printed and ICT-based
     information texts: 4a,c

ACTIVITIES AND APPROACHES

Introducing and investigating the script

Extract A from the playscript can be used in several ways. Read it as a class, mime in groups with the pupils in role and/or action narrate with the whole group as spectators. The pupils need to investigate the text and search for clues about the characters, story and setting. This can be done through discussion and/or presented in the form of a spidergram.

Samacs and Bretevs

From their reading of extract B, pupils use the 'role(s) on the wall' convention to identify the different characteristics of the Samacs and the Bretevs. It is also possible to do this on screen, especially if a projector is available, so that text can be moved, manipulated, stored and altered.

The pupils then, in groups, produce two visual images (still pictures / freeze-frames) to represent the different characteristics (an image of a Bretev and an image of a Samac).

Introducing an alternative perspective
Links with Kosovo

Ask the pupils to freeze the above images. While they do so, read out the web site page: 'What it's like being a Serb' (http://www.khao.org/articles002.htm) but substitute Samacs, Bretevs and other names to 'hide' the actual references in the text (see below as a guide):

It's embarrassing being a ~~Serb~~ [Samac] these days. When I venture out of my ever-shrinking homeland it gets harder and harder to hold my head high. Early this year a ~~Serb~~ [Samac] friend and I went to Mali to see the famous Dogon Cliff dwellings. But when other foreigners visiting there found out who we were, we became the tourist attraction. 'What are you doing here?' they'd ask. What they really meant was, shouldn't you be driving Muslims from their homes and shelling defenseless villages?' I was in ~~Tangiers~~ [another country] when my ~~Bosnian Serb~~ [Samac] cousins overran ~~Srebrenica~~ and slaughtered its menfolk. Feelings agains ~~Serbs~~ [Samacs] ran so high that I had to pretend to be a ~~Bulgarian~~ [foreigner]. Unfortunately, the famous ~~Bulgarian~~ national football team was quite well known ~~in Morocco~~, and I couldn't even name the starting players. I had to pose as a ~~Croat~~ [Bretev] instead. The worst thing was, I couldn't help but agree with my ~~Arab~~ critics. I certainly have never condoned what our would-be president-for-life, ~~Slobodan Milosevic~~, has done in his ruthless pursuit of personal power. But collective guilt is hard to escape.

TEACHING AND LEARNING COMMENTARY

By exploring these two pages in these ways, pupils begin to select and sort the relevant information. They also begin to take a real interest in the material and want to know more. Using extracts in this way, not beginning at the start of texts, is a good way of capturing the pupils' interest quickly.

The use of the still pictures allows pupils to think further about the words they have just used on the 'role on the wall'. This convention enables them to select and combine particular ideas.

This is a very powerful piece of text. It can be altered before the lesson so that you find it straightforward to read. Personal accounts from more recent events can also be used in this way.

NC/NLS REFERENCES

EN1 Drama: 4a,b,c
Listening: 9c
Group discussion: 10a

EN1 Drama: 4a
EN3 Composition: 1c,d,e,f,g,h,l,n
Planning and drafting: 2c
Handwriting and presentation: 5c
Breadth of study: 8, 9

ACTIVITIES AND APPROACHES

Betrayal

Ask the pupils to read extract C in pairs. Then, as a whole group, watch a pair. Stop the drama at 'MY POTATOES' and ask the pupils to think about what the characters would say or think next. When they have made suggestions ask them to stand behind the character for whom they have spoken. Once several pupils (or all the pupils) have made suggestions and have stood behind the appropriate characters, re-run the scene, this time hearing the communal voices.

Placing 'texts' within the drama

Different activities can be developed where the pupils are able to produce pieces of 'text' that are 'added' to the drama. For example, if the pupils 'move' into the house and set up the characters in a still picture, perhaps with the box, then a blank piece of paper can be held up in various positions while the pupils are asked what would be on this piece of paper. Depending on where the piece of paper is positioned, they will make different suggestions as to what may appear on it. If it is held above the characters' heads, they might suggest it is a picture or a certificate. Placed in one of the character's hands, in an envelope or screwed up and thrown at their feet, they will suggest something different. The pupils are then asked to create pieces of text that can appear in any of these places. It is important that they create two identical versions.

ICT can, therefore, be a useful tool here. If the pupils need more guidance then a variety of pre-prepared templates could be made available on the computer (posters, war images, certificates, letters, etc.) or the pupils could create these themselves. Of course, it is equally possible for pupils to draw and write these without a computer, but this is a situation that lends itself to fully integrating the use of ICT within the work.

When the pupils have completed the pieces of 'text', the pieces of paper are placed in the scene. This might be a good opportunity for the teacher to be in role so that they are able to respond to some of the 'texts'. The characters can then read and respond to the pieces of paper placed around them. At this stage, the teacher might also use this opportunity to introduce another piece of paper (a conscription letter, a war recruitment poster, a letter, etc). Other scenes where text could be added are in the drill hall or a recruitment office.

Return to the text from the 'What it's like being a Serb' web site and reveal the real identity.

TEACHING AND LEARNING COMMENTARY

Forum theatre can be used here to encourage pupils to think about the characters' reactions, intention, actions and ideas – through the suggestions that they make and the discussion that takes place.

By introducing pieces of text here, pupils not only progress in the drama but develop language skills that are relevant to the rest of the English curriculum and beyond.

The technique of adding text to the drama can be used in many different situations. It helps pupils to develop the drama at the same time that they are having to think about the language, style and format needed for specific pieces of text for specific audiences. It is also a useful way for pupils to 'place' texts in a historical or social context as they have to think carefully about these aspects.

NC/NLS REFERENCES

EN1 Drama: 4a,b,c
EN2 Printed and ICT-based
     information texts: 4a,b,c
EN2 Non-fiction and non-literary
     texts: 9b

EN1 Drama: 4a,b,c,d
     Speaking: 1a,b,c
EN2 Printed and ICT-based
     information texts: 4a,b,c,d
     Non-fiction and non-literary
     texts: 9b
EN3: Composition: 1
      Planning and drafting: 2
      Handwriting and
      presentation: 5
      Breadth of study: 8, 9

ACTIVITIES AND APPROACHES

E-mails From Kosovo

In January 1998, while the world heard reports of a massacre and renewed fighting in Yugoslavia, a 16-year-old girl (under the pseudonym Adona) began e-mailing her experiences of living in the middle of a war zone to Finnegan Hamill a high school student in Berkeley, California. Unedited excerpts of the e-mails are reproduced on the web site:
http://CNN.com/SPECIALS/1998/10/kosovo/email/archive.html

A variety of drama activities and conventions can be used with this material. The chronological order of the e-mails in Parts I–III can be used to develop 'performances' that explore the factual depictions, or imagery, of the e-mails. If different groups are given the three different sets of e-mails, a series of images can be developed in this way and the pupils can link in the previous images of the Samacs and Bretevs. This allows the pupils to use many of the conventions that they have developed in this work and create links between the different elements of the drama. The mask work can again be used so that the pupils replace masks with the 'faces' depicted, either through symbolic drama or the realisation of the events.

The pupils then hold their final images (freeze the image) while the teacher reads the transcript of the telephone conversation between Finnegan and Adona in Part IV.

Placing 'texts' within the drama

As above, pieces of 'text' can be added to this work. The scene can be set up where Adona is collecting her papers together and they are packing ready to move out. The blank piece of paper can be used and the teacher can, if necessary, take on a role to respond in role to the 'texts' created.

Further work could be developed from the e-mails, the 'What it's like being a Serb' text and/or other material available on the web sites. A variety of situations could be developed with the teacher in role as, for example, a NATO officer offering the refugees a chance to go abroad with only a limited number of places available, or helping them to find members of their family.

Further texts could be introduced into the drama (letters asking for help in finding their families, newspaper articles, etc.).

Some web sites to investigate:
www. antiwar.com   www.zmag.org
www.gov.yu   http://www.bg.ac.yu
http://www.serbia-info.com   www.nato.int
http://www.kosovapress.com/english/index.htm

TEACHING AND LEARNING COMMENTARY

By this stage, pupils are able to work independently to develop the drama. Using the techniques that they have been developing throughout, they can begin to explore the e-mails in a number of different dramatic ways. You should set out the structure of the work by giving clear instructions about the final image and the use of the two e-mails, but within that structure the pupils can begin to use a variety of techniques, symbolic or otherwise, to explore the material.

These final images and other aspect of the drama that have been created can be brought together with a variety of extracts from the texts to conclude the unit of work. You can decide which images the pupils can end with and which text (the extracts from the *Bretevski Street* playscript, 'What it's like being a Serb' or the e-mails) is most suited to being read at the end of the work.

You will see from the work on Kosovo the ways that drama and ICT can be used to explore a variety of texts, issues, themes and ideas. The suggestions are not supposed to be rigid and can be adapted to suit the particular class you are teaching by selecting and adapting the various choices. What should be apparent is that many of these ideas, techniques and approaches can be used with a variety of other texts, issues or recent events.

Resource 12b

EXTRACT A

CORMAC: I did the beans for you, tied them all up.

ISOBEL examines the beans.

ISOBEL: That's good. (She looks around the garden.) We used to have honeysuckle years ago, and when it began to get hot, like this, early in the morning you could smell it all over the house. Everything tasted of it, even the bread Granny made.

Hortense enters and hangs some washing on the line.

HORTENSE: Stop gossiping about me, I know what you're up to.

CORMAC: We've still to a packet of seeds from last year, look.

ISOBEL: One packet of seeds isn't going to feed us Cormac.

Cormac throws the seeds back in the shed.

ISOBEL: Maybe you're right, we should plant them. How do we usually do it?

CORMAC: I make holes and you put them in.

ISOBEL: That's right, I remember.

ISOBEL and CORMAC kneel down and sow the seeds together.

HORTENSE: That's how your mother and I used to sow the seeds when she was a little girl. It's tradition.

CORMAC: I've got to go to Brigade.

HORTENSE: Give your Grandmother a hug then, or I'll hide my false teeth in your bed tonight.

CORMAC: You haven't got false teeth.

HORTENSE: I shall have to borrow some then.

CORMAC gives HORTENSE a hug and then he goes.

HORTENSE kneels down and helps ISOBEL with sowing the seeds.

HORTENSE: You don't cuddle that child enough Isobel.

ISOBEL: Oh really? I don't remember you being big on hugging when we were children.

HORTENSE: It was my loss.

ISOBEL exits to the house. HORTENSE exits in the opposite direction.

Later that night.

ISOBEL comes out and begins to take in the washing.

PIERRE and VAS are in their garden digging, they do not know that ISOBEL can overhear them.

PIERRE: Give me the rest of the potatoes Vas.

VAS hands over the potatoes and helps PIERRE by shining a torch onx the ground. PIERRE continues digging.

PIERRE: They keep better if you bury them, stops them rotting.

ISOBEL exits.

PIERRE covers up the potatoes and now moves to another part of the garden.

PIERRE: Come on Vas. Vas!

VAS: I don't see why we have to hide Mum's things as well.

PIERRE: You want them to be safe, don't you? What if someone broke into the house and stole them? What would we do then?

VAS: You never worried about that before.

PIERRE: Things are different now.

VAS: I want to keep them, they've always been in my room.

PIERRE: Vas, after the war you can keep them for ever, I promise. Now come on.

VAS hands over the box with his mother's things and PIERRE buries it.

Machine gun fire answered by sniper shots.

EXTRACT B

HORTENSE: We ate mice in the war.

PIERRE: Hortense!

HORTENSE: We ate everything. They found a child in St Varnese all alone. She'd eaten the lino off the floor.

The boule game continues. Hortense and Pierre stand quietly for a moment in the garden.

PIERRE: It's strangely quiet today.

They listen

 Maybe I'm just imagining it.

They play.

HORTENSE: I remember this town when the Samacs had it, before you were born. I lived through it. I'd rather be dead in the ground than let them back in. I mean it Pierre. We won't be safe until they're all dead, everyone.

PIERRE: Hortense, you don't mean that.

HORTENSE: I do Pierre. You haven't seen what they did, in the last war. Terrible things, terrible.

PIERRE: That's war Hortense, everyone did terrible things.

HORTENSE: It's in their blood. Murder.

PIERRE: And I suppose the Virgin Mary told you that.

HORTENSE: How dare you insult the Holy Virgin.

PIERRE: What about the children? Aren't they like any other children? Aren't they just like Cormac?

HORTENSE: You know what they did to my husband ...

PIERRE: Yes but Hortense...

HORTENSE: They weren't going to kill him, to have killed him would have been too kind ...

CORMAC enters in his brigade uniform unseen and listens.

PIERRE: Hortense ...

HORTENSE: Eight brave Samac soldiers standing in this garden, standing on my husband, firing bullets in his knees and in his ankles, in his elbows and his wrists. They took away my husband that night and the man I got back hobbled around this garden for the next six years watering the flowers with his tears. I'd love it if they were all dead, love it, rejoice in it.

CORMAC exits, as Pierre stares at him in his uniform.

EXTRACT C

PIERRE enters and sits drinking in his garden.

PIERRE: When did you steal them Isobel? Did you sneak over in the night and dig them up ever so quietly?

ISOBEL: Getting drunk's a very clever thing to do.

PIERRE: Don't tell me how to behave.

ISOBEL: Who do you think you are, God almighty? Your soul isn't so clean Pierre.

PIERRE: Really? Did you have any particular sins in mind I wonder?

ISOBEL: I told you we were eating grass and you pretended you had no food left while you had potatoes buried in your garden.

PIERRE: Yes, MY POTATOES.

Unit 13

History, gender and power: using drama to explore a historical context

This unit, which focuses on the story of 'Bessy Dunlop: Witch of Dalry', deals with issues of gender and power in the context of the 'witchcraze' in mediaeval Britain. It draws on real historical contexts and, as such, covers a wide range of texts including some powerful, pre-1914, non-literary texts and contemporary script.

Resources

Anonymous poem dedicated to women who suffered as 'witches'

Source documents of the witchcraze in Europe – non-literary texts (contemporary and pre-twentieth century

Various item which set the character of Bessy Dunlop: shawl, herbs, wicker basket, small pot

Sugar paper, pens, pencils

Learning objectives

The lesson will provide opportunities for pupils to develop their skills as speakers and listeners (En1) by working in role as members of a village, readers (En2) by reading source documents on witchcraft and writers (En3) by writing letters of petition in role.

Extracts from the units …

Set up two figures in the room at either end of the class – one to represent Bessy and the other the laird. Ask the pupils, in role as villagers, to consider what the laird has said and decide which person they will support and to stand beside them.

Commentary:
This exercise should be introduced with a discussion about the implications of going against the wishes of the laird – who was all-powerful.

NC REFERENCES	ACTIVITIES AND APPROACHES	TEACHING AND LEARNING COMMENTARY
	## Phase 1: setting the scene	
En2 Texts from different cultures and traditions: 3a,b Media and moving image texts: 5a,b,c,d En1 Group discussion and interaction: 3a,b,c,d,e	Establish a classroom setting that allows pupils to both collaborate in small groups and to feed back to the whole group. Begin by displaying the word 'Witch' and ask pupils to respond to it to gauge their modern associations of the word.	The word 'witch' will have many connections and associations, and 'airing' these at this point will allow you to explore the superstitions and prejudices it generates.
	Organise pupils into pairs or small groups and ask them to study the picture of the three witches hanging from the gibbet (resource 13a) and come to an agreement about: • what they can see • what they find disturbing • the possible reason for this execution.	Your classroom might be organised around discussion tables at this time with a space to convene in the middle. Pupils are again encouraged to speculate openly about the text to provoke their thinking on the subject.
En1 Speaking: 1a	After a few minutes, ask one member of each group to feed back their comments. Using a volunteer as a scribe, collect these responses on sugar paper. Keep the responses for later.	Keeping the responses will allow you to re-visit initial impressions for discussion and reflection.
En1 Standard English: 5 Language variation: 6a Group discussion and interaction: 10a,b	Introduce the anonymous poem (resource 13a) to the group by first moving everyone into a circle. Ask the group to accept you, as teacher, in the role of an archaeologist who has discovered a document found buried at the site of a witch hanging that took place in the Middle Ages. In role, narrate the poem to the group (possibly give them a copy to follow) and then place them in role as co-investigators whose task is to uncover the reasons someone may have had for writing such a poem.	The use of teacher-in-role at this stage models what is expected from the pupils and it allows the teacher to adopt a style of 'academic' language – the objectivity of a professional inquiry.
En1 Drama: 4a	The teacher's role might start with the question: *As archaeologists investigating this document, what can we say happened to women accused of witchcraft?*	The work in role establishes the plight of women as a serious issue of investigation. (With an inexperienced group, you may need to step in and out of role in order to establish the conventions of group meetings, e.g. taking turns, using appropriate language, speculating, listening, etc.)
En1 Group discussion and interaction: 3e	Provide pupils with the list of possible theories for the witchcraze (resource 13b). Ask them to read it in groups and to form their own preferred reasoning. After a short time, ask them to reconvene and feed back their findings in role as archaeologists.	Further speculation serves to heighten pupil interest and leads on to the specific drama activity concerning Bessy herself.
En1 Speaking: 1a,b Listening: 2a,b	Working out of role, ask the group what questions their investigation has raised about women and the witchcraze. Keep a record of their questions.	The group has now encountered the issues of the witchcraze, considered its effect on women, speculated about its causes and developed some tentative theories.

NC/NLS REFERENCES	ACTIVITIES AND APPROACHES	TEACHING AND LEARNING COMMENTARY

Meeting Bessy Dunlop

En1 Drama activities: 11a

To establish the role of Bessy Dunlop, a healer in the Scottish village of Dalry in medieval Scotland, you will need to provide a few simple props, e.g. a wicker basket, a shawl, some dried herbs and a pot.

These items are merely to signify the change of role to the group. They may help to fix the idea for both you, as teacher-in-role, and the class.

Before moving into role, tell the group that the owner of these objects was hanged as a witch in the seventeenth century. Then, move into role by sitting on the floor and placing various herbs into the pot.

The second teacher-in-role strategy should be effective because the pupils are now experienced and the objects act as a focus of interest. Pupils need to be encouraged to ask questions before the role begins.

En1 Drama: 4a

As this hot-seat unfolds, Bessy needs to impart the following information to the group:

I am known as a healer in my village. I know many things about herbs and many villagers come from far and wide for cures to such things as toothaches, childhood sicknesses and fevers. I am also the midwife and I have delivered most of the children in this village. Although my husband is now dead, I have my own house and land.

It is important to establish Bessy as a woman of some stature within the village because her ultimate plight stems partly from her knowledge and power.

En1 Drama activities: 11a

The pupils can now be invited to meet Bessy in role as villagers who have come to her with ailments or problems for her to solve.

Step forward and tell me what ails you.

This widening of the roles allows pupils to participate actively and to directly experience the status of Bessy.

Bessy's dilemma

En1 Listening: 2a

Out of role, tell the group about Bessy's most serious problem. She has heard through gossip in the village that the laird's wilful daughter, Marie, has been seeing one of the farmhands on Bessy's farm, against her father's wishes.

This situation has the double advantage of being both a modern and very ancient problem.

Begin a gossip circle with the whole group passing around the rumour about Marie and the farm boy.

This allows all of the class to experience the vicarious thrill of the rumour mill.

En1 Drama: 4a

Ask for a volunteer to take on Marie's role as she comes to Bessy for a consultation:

My father wants to marry me to the laird of Oban's son but he is a weak and haughty man who does not please me. I love Jimmy who works on Bessy's farm and I want him for my man.

This could also operate as a piece of paired improvisation. Be sure to tell the group to explore the argument without Marie ever changing her mind.

The laird's revenge

En1 Drama: 4a
En1 Listening: 2b,f

Still out of role, read out the decree that has been issued by the laird when he found out that Bessy has been 'meddling' in the affairs of his family and 'turning his daughter against him', as he sees it.

At this stage, the suggestion of witchery is planted by the laird as a first step towards outright accusation.

Cracking Drama © NATE Drama Committee 2000

NC/NLS REFERENCES

ACTIVITIES AND APPROACHES

TEACHING AND LEARNING COMMENTARY

NC/NLS REFERENCES	ACTIVITIES AND APPROACHES	TEACHING AND LEARNING COMMENTARY
	Be it known that the woman, Bessy, has turned my child against me with the potions and her charms. No man in my employ is to have further dealings with her. Anyone so doing will have to leave the village.	
En1 Group discussion and interaction: 3a,b,c,d,e	Discuss what Bessy might do about this development.	
En1 Drama: 4a	Set up two figures in the room at either end of the class – one to represent Bessy and the other the laird. Ask the pupils, in role as villagers, to consider what the laird has said and decide which person they will support and to stand beside them.	This exercise should be introduced with a discussion about the implications of going against the wishes of the laird – who was all-powerful.
En1 Drama: 4a	Discuss with the class how people might now begin to treat Bessy. Improvise some of the suggestions.	This is quite open-ended and pupils may come up with a wide variety of possible reactions: some supporting Bessy and others against her.
En1 Drama: 4a	Choose one person from the class who seems to have changed his/her response to Bessy from initial support to condemnations. Set up the 'angel-on-the-shoulder' technique, e.g. CHARACTER: *Bessy Dunlop made my baby fall sick and die. She's evil.* DEVIL: *This should get me in the laird's good books.* ANGEL: *Bessy did all she could for my baby daughter.*	This explores the inner conflict of the role and begins to chart the process of accusation that leads finally to the persecution of Bessy.
En1 Group discussion and interaction: 3a,b,c,d,e Group discussion and interaction: 10a,b En2 Understanding texts: 1a,b,c,d English literary heritage: 2a Non-fiction and non-literary texts: 9a	Return to the poem, the theories and the groups' original responses to the word 'Witch' and to the witchcraze. Ask the pupils to identify why people behave like this to one another. Can they think of modern parallels to the witchcraze? How can such injustices be prevented?	This reflective section of the project asks pupils to make some links between the mediaeval and the modern worlds and to explore issues of morality, gender roles and abuse of power.

For all those who died – stripped
naked, shorn.

For all those who screamed in pain
to the Great Goddess, only to have their
tongues ripped out by the root.

For those who were pricked, racked, broken on
the wheel for the sins of their Inquisitors.

For all those whose beauty stripped their
torturers to fury; and for those whose
ugliness did the same.

For all those who were neither ugly nor
beautiful, but only women who would not
submit.

For all those quick fingers, broken in the vice.

For all those soft arms, pulled from their sockets.

For all those budding breasts, ripped with
hot pincers.

For all those midwives, killed merely for the
sin of delivering man to an imperfect world.

For all those witch-women, my sisters, who
breathed freer as the flames took them, knowing
as they shed their female bodies, the seared
flesh falling like fruit in the flames,
that death alone would cleanse them
of the sin for which they died – the sin
of being born a woman who is more than
the sum of her parts.

(Anonymous, sixteenth century)

Resource 13b

Theories about witchcraft

At least four major interpretations of European witchcraft are current. The first is the old liberal view that witchcraft never existed at all but was a monstrous invention by the ecclesiastical authorities in order to enhance their powers and enlarge their purses. For this school, the history of witchcraft is a chapter in the history of repression and inhumanity.

The second tradition is the folklorist or Murrayite tradition ... Murray argued that European witchcraft was an ancient fertility religion based on the worship of the horned god Dianus.

A third school, currently the most influential, emphasises the social history of witchcraft, especially the social pattern of witch accusations.

A fourth group of historians emphasises the history of ideas and argues that witchcraft is a composite of concepts gradually assembled over the centuries. Of these, Christian heresy and theology are more important than paganism.

(from Jeffrey B. Russell, *A History of Witchcraft: Sorcerers, Heretics and Pagans,* Thames and Hudson, 1980)

Unit 14

Links and layers: active approaches to comparing pre-twentieth and twentieth-century texts

This unit explores the following three texts:

- 'The Signal Man' by Charles Dickens
- 'The Call' by Robert Westall
- 'A Basket Full of Wallpaper' by Colum McCann (from *Headless* English and Media Centre Publications)

The approaches to these texts, from the use of drama conventions to 'formal' essay writing for the GCSE English assignment, should not be seen separately but should complement each other so that pupils (and the teacher) can make clear links between them. The practical work leads to a more detailed analysis and understanding of the stories and the drama process. The essays are very much informed by the practical work and analysis that has gone before them. Suggested titles can be found on page 98.

Resources

Copies of the texts listed above

A variety of props/objects relevant to the three stories (see the sections 'Strange but True' in each case)

Learning objectives

Pupils often find it difficult to make links between texts, particularly when they need to move away from thematic links to explore structure, language and style. The approaches outlined below show how, through drama, these links can be successfully explored by pupils, allowing them to come to a greater understanding of the narrative structures, styles and the writers' techniques as well as the thematic, content-based similarities that exist. Through this process, pupils will develop their analytical skills as well as the ability to transfer this critical thinking to other texts, ideas or issues. Although some of the approaches suggested below are related to the individual texts, the repetition of ideas, conventions and techniques and the deliberately active nature of them should mean that pupils begin to find links (guided by the teacher) and move away from a purely narrative approach. The use of role, visual image and dramatic conventions should, therefore, play a central part in this.

Extracts from the units ...

During several of the above activities, particularly when still pictures are being used, pupils can be asked to place the narrator in the picture, as storyteller and/or character narrator. Pupils are then given a chance to move the narrator according to their distance from certain characters, the events, the reader's view, what control the narrator has, etc. The reader can be placed in the picture in the same way, and the space between the reader and the narrator described. This works particularly well with 'The Call' because of the different layers of narration that exist (the rota secretary, The log-book, etc.).

Commentary:

This can be used throughout the work to reinforce the thinking about the role of the narrators throughout the stories. By physically placing the narrator and/or reader in the picture, pupils question the style, language and authorial control as well as discuss what the reader brings with her/him to the story. Such work has a direct effect on their ability to write about this and use evidence from the text to back up their ideas.

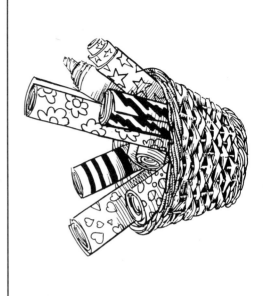

NC REFERENCES	ACTIVITIES AND APPROACHES	TEACHING AND LEARNING COMMENTARY

Creating links … using all three texts together

A possible opening: beginning at the end!

NC REFERENCES

EN1 Speaking: 8a,b
Listening: 9c
Group discussion and interaction: 10a

EN2 Understanding texts: 1a.g. h,i,k

ACTIVITIES

Before the pupils read any of the stories, present them with information about the three deaths (one from each story), either in the form of newspaper reports, witness statements or the findings of an inquest. This could then lead to a variety of prediction and analytical exercises where the pupils are given clues and take on the role of the investigator/researcher (see 'Strange but True' below). This encourages them to analyse the texts in detail as they search for information and also helps to overcome some of the language barriers that might exist with 'The Signalman'.

TEACHING AND LEARNING COMMENTARY

This work can be approached in a number of different ways. If the pupils are to take on specific roles, time will need to be spent developing these. Giving the pupils additional short extracts from the stories helps them to begin to explore the text and its features in detail and, even at this early stage, begin to make links between the texts.

Strange but True

EN1 Drama: 4a,b
Drama activities: 11a
Speaking: 8a,b,c
Listening: 9a,c
Group discussion and interaction: 10a

EN2 Understanding texts: 1a,b,c,d
Media and moving image texts: 5c,k

Explain to the group that you are going to be in-role as the TV producer of the programme *Strange but True*. Six pupils (two for each story) are given short extracts from the stories and some relevant items (see below for examples). These six pupils are to be interviewed by the researchers about the strange events and, therefore, take on an 'expert' role. The rest of the pupils are researchers for the programme.

It is important that the roles are clearly established. This activity gives the pupils a specific need to develop questioning skills and analyse information, both oral and from the text. The context means that pupils quickly establish the 'mystery' nature of the stories and, through their own understanding of the genre, begin to search for specific clues.

Examples of objects to be given to the six pupils

The Signalman	The Call	A Basket Full of Wallpaper
Newspaper reports/headlines	Samaritans' log-book	Rolls of wallpaper
Signalman's flag	Samaritans' information leaflets	Paper dolls
A whistle	Christmas stocking	Beach pebbles
Extract from video of *The Signalman*	Dog lead	Information on Japan and/or Hiroshima
Picture of the signalman and/or the tunnel	Weather forecast – fog	£20 note or something that looks like one

The need to choose a theme or title for the programme means that the pupils need to develop links between the texts. Although at this stage these are often thematic, the analysis required encourages them to question the authorial voice and language used.

Issues are raised about the nature of such programmes, the aims of the producer and researcher, types of questioning and the use of 'facts', artefacts and fiction.

These roles can be developed/re-visited throughout the work and could, if time permits, lead to completion of the programme.

The producer outlines the information about the three deaths in the form of reports, letters, statements, etc. and explains to the researchers that s/he wants all three stories to appear on the same programme if enough 'strange' information can be discovered and if a link can be established between them. The producer also explains that they need some good photographs, to show

NC/NLS REFERENCES

ACTIVITIES AND APPROACHES

TEACHING AND LEARNING COMMENTARY

as backdrops to the story or to help with the re-enactment and/or some relevant artefacts. The researchers are sent under a strict time limit (the deadline for beginning production is very soon!) to discover what they can.

A production meeting is subsequently held to pull together the findings. The pupils being interviewed should also be asked how they felt about being interviewed and whether the stories had remained as they had told them to the researchers. The production meeting needs to arrive at a theme/title for the programme that links the stories.

Matching pairs

EN1 Drama: 4a,b,d
EN2 Understanding texts: 1a,b,c,k

Divide the pupils into pairs and give each pair a sentence/phrase from one of the three stories (using different coloured paper or card to distinguish their sources). Ask each pair to stand in an area of the room allocated to the relevant story, e.g.

```
The                The Call          A Basket Full
Signalman                            of Wallpaper
```

The pupils read out their sentences/extracts in turn. From memory, they then have to link up with a pair from another story that they think fits with theirs. The pupils read out the extracts again, linking them together in some way and explaining the link.

The pairs move back to their original places. This time they produce a still picture to fit their sentence/extract. All pupils are given a chance to see everyone's still pictures and then have to match their own image up with one by another pair. The links created this time are often different, which (usually) leads to an interesting discussion!

This activity can be adapted in a number of ways. For example, the still pictures from one story can be held while the extract from the other story is read out. The same activity can also be used for each individual story to show the links, and repeated writer's techniques that exist within each.

If this is approached very much like a game of 'pairs', the pupils soon search for links. Often, during this activity, they begin moving away from the thematic links to more 'obscure' links – water imagery used in both, the use of particular words, the lack of communication, etc.

By moving on to the use of still pictures to create links, the pupils are further encouraged to analyse the text in detail. They begin to explore character and the visual images that exist either directly or indirectly (imagery) throughout the text. The discussion and explanations that take place encourage pupils to develop their ability to find quotations and evidence from the text to back up their ideas.

NC/NLS REFERENCES

ACTIVITIES AND APPROACHES

TEACHING AND LEARNING COMMENTARY

Layers of wallpaper (or pupils!)

The image left at the end of 'A Basketful of Wallpaper' of the layers of wallpaper in Osobe's house provides a useful way of exploring all three stories.

The idea of layers is a useful way of exploring both text and drama. By getting the pupils to actually represent these layers by standing in lines and moving according to the discussions that take place, they begin to question and understand the relationships that exist between writer, reader and text.

EN2 Understanding texts: 1a,b,c,g,h,i

Rolls of wallpaper can be used to explore the different layers that exist in the stories so that the pupils can explore how the layers are developed and how, at times they are covered up and at other times are revealed, etc. Writing key words or sentences on the sheets of wallpaper allows the pupils to do this and creates links between the stories showing how the authors build up the layers.

Another useful method is to use rows of pupils to represent the different layers of wallpaper. This can be approached in several different ways. For example, ask groups of pupils (three separate groups with one task each) to decide:

The critical analysis required for this activity encourages pupils to develop high-order reading skills in terms of recognising the authorial voice. This has a direct effect on their writing when they produce the critical essays towards the end of the work.

- what they *definitely* know about the characters or events in the story/stories
- what they *think* they know or (relating it to the assignment) what is *imagined*
- what they would *like to believe / what they would like to know.*

EN2 Understanding texts: 1a,b,c,d,g,h,i,j

The pupils, each representing one thing, then move into the three different layers to represent the different layers of the story/stories. They can either call out what they know, imagine or like to know (leading to movement between the different layers through discussion) or they can present still pictures representing the different layers. Once the layers of the story have been decided on, the pupils then have to decide which layer is at the front according to:

You need to think carefully about the extracts that are read out. For example, an extract is more useful if it includes *two* different types of narration or where the reader takes a *more active role.*

- the chronological order of the story
- the reader's final view
- the writers' intentions.

EN1 Listening: 2b,f; 9c

Group discussion and interaction: 3a,b

If extracts of the story/stories are then read out (or even the whole story) the pupils (or layers) have to move when they feel another layer of the story is revealed or covered up.

This leads to some very interesting discussions about narrative structure/techniques as the pupils feel that, by moving, they are in many ways 'being' the narrator and/or writer.

Many different layers can be created, for example layers of:

- narration (writer, narrative method, narrator as character)
- time (past, present, predictions)
- suspense
- visual images (description, imagination).

This activity can work particularly well with 'A Basketful of Wallpaper' to show the different layers of Osobe's life: the pupils select different sentences or words from the stories and then form different lines to represent the different layers.

NC/NLS REFERENCES	ACTIVITIES AND APPROACHES	TEACHING AND LEARNING COMMENTARY
	Remember that pupils can be asked to move the layers according to different parts of the story, a character's view of the events, etc. – and if you don't want all this activity, then use the wallpaper sheets instead!	
	Telling the story	
EN1 Drama: 4a,b Drama activities: 11a Speaking 1a,b,c; 8a Listening: 2a,b,f; 9 a Group discussion and interaction: 3a; 10a	Organise the pupils into groups of four or five, sitting in a circle facing each other. Ask one person in each group to begin telling the story from memory. When the teacher calls 'Next!', the next person in the circle has to carry on telling the story. The pupils can then be asked to tell the story as if they were one of the characters in the story (not the narrator) – the landlord; Geoff, Meg, Tom or Harry; Osobe, the father, a villager. Actions can be brought in and/or other pupils can be asked to act out the events while the story is being told.	This activity can be repeated at different stages throughout the work. It is a good way of overcoming any problems with the language, getting the stories clear in pupils' minds and thinking about the different narrative methods.
	Moment of crisis or tension	
EN1 Drama: 4a,b Drama activities: 11a Speaking 1a,b,d EN2 Understanding texts: 1a,c,g,k	Ask the pupils, in groups, to create a still picture depicting the moment of crisis or tension within the story, using a sentence from the text to accompany the picture. If the pupils produce one for each story they can then be asked to rearrange the sentences to fit with one of the other images. Alternatively, if different groups have different stories, one group can be asked to place their sentence on another group's picture.	By establishing the moment of crisis/tension in this way, pupils have to analyse the text and consider the use of authorial control in establishing suspense. Placing the sentence from one story with a still picture from another encourages pupils to develop comparative skills.
	A similar activity can be developed if pupils, in groups, select three to five significant images from a story and present them as a tableau using sentences from the text to accompany the images. The mixing of images and sentences can then take place and/or a discussion about the order of the pictures and whether or not this can be changed.	
	Positioning the narrator	
EN1 Drama: 4a,b,d EN2 Understanding texts: 1i,j,k	During several of the above activities, particularly when still pictures are being used, pupils can be asked to place the narrator in the picture, as storyteller and/or character narrator. Pupils are then given a chance to move the narrator in according to their distance from certain characters, the events, etc. The reader's view, what control the narrator has, etc. The reader can be placed in the picture in the same way, and the space between the reader and the narrator described. This works particularly well with 'The Call' because of the different layers of narration that exist (the rota secretary, the log-book, etc.).	This can be used throughout the work to reinforce the thinking about the role of the narrators throughout the stories. By physically placing the narrator and/or reader in the picture, pupils question the style, language and authorial control as well as discuss what the reader brings with her/him to the story. Such work has a direct effect on their ability to write about this and use evidence from the text to back up their ideas.
	Imagination tracking	
EN1 Drama: 4a,b,d EN2 Understanding texts: 1a,b,c,g,k	During several of the above activities, thought-tracking can be used. Because of the nature of the three stories, however, it is also possible to track the imagination of the characters. Ask the pupils to *describe* what a character is imagining at any time during the story, or *present a picture* of this, and compare	Where a thought tunnel can be used (e.g. as the Samaritan leaves to find his wife, he walks through a tunnel of pupils who, one by one, express his thoughts), the teacher can adapt this slightly to present images of what is imagined.

Cracking Drama © NATE Drama Committee 2000

ACTIVITIES AND APPROACHES

TEACHING AND LEARNING COMMENTARY

this with what is being said or the 'real' events that are taking place. This process helps the pupils think about the power of imagination and the ways that all three writers build it into their stories.

The individual stories
'The Signalman'

The beginning and the end

EN1   Drama: 4a,b,d
       Drama activities: 11a

Present pupils with the beginning and the end of the story (on an A4 sheet). Organise the pupils into groups and ask them to find one sentence from the opening and one sentence from the end that they could represent by the same still picture. Each group shows its still picture to the rest of the class, who have to guess the two lines they have chosen. A further two lines could then be chosen by each group and the still pictures created. This should start pupils thinking about the different ways that visual images are used/created.

The aim is to follow a similar approach to each story. Read parts of the story at a time.

Because the mysterious nature of 'The Signalman' is dependent on the visual image created at the beginning and end of the story, this activity is a good way to establish this and an easy way of breaking down any concerns about the language. It also moves them away from the thematic to a more detailed understanding of language, imagery and authorial purpose.

The first conversation

EN1   Drama: 4a,b,d
       Drama activities: 11a

Read the first part of the story, as far as:

... To such purpose I spoke to him; but I am far from sure of the terms I used; for, besides that I am not happy in opening any conversation, there was something in the man that daunted me.

Ask pairs of pupils to work in role to create the conversation they think took place when the narrator and the signalman first meet.

If the pupils are asked during this work to take one still picture from the scene that links with the text elsewhere, it encourages them to build up comparisons and helps them to avoid, later, writing about these scenes as if Dickens wrote them.

The past

EN1   Drama: 4a,b,d
       Drama activities: 11a

EN2   Understanding texts:
       1a,b,c,g,k

Read on, as far as:

He had been a pupil of natural philosophy ... It was far too late to make another.

Ask the pupils, in groups, to create a scene from the signalman's past life as a pupil. During the scenes, are they able to produce any *visual images, language* or *ideas* that link in with the story so far or their work on the beginning and end of the story?

The pupils, by working in role, begin to consider the characters within the stories.

Back at the inn

EN1   Drama: 4a,
       Drama activities: 11a

Read on, as far as:

... and I got back to my inn without any adventure.

Ask the pupils to recreate the scene at the inn that night.

This could provide a good opportunity for whole-class drama with the teacher in role as the narrator asking questions and being given information, etc. The pupils will need to think carefully about their roles, which provides you with an opportunity to focus on the period of the story as well as the social/cultural setting.

NC/NLS REFERENCES

EN1 Drama: 4a
EN2 Understanding texts: 1a,d,g,k

EN1 Drama: 4a

EN1 Drama: 4a,
Drama activities: 11a

EN2 Understanding texts: 1a,c,g

EN1 Drama: 4a
EN2 Understanding texts: 1a

ACTIVITIES AND APPROACHES

Significant sentences and scenes
Read on, as far as:

I had offered to stay through the night, but he would not hear of it.

Ask the pupils, in groups, to choose between six and ten significant sentences in the story so far. They should present these sentences in a 'tableau' effect. One member of the group could narrate, or each sentence could be spoken by a different character in turn.

Back at the inn 2
The scene back at the inn can be recreated once again to discuss the events that the narrator now knows about (see above).

The end
Read to the end of the story. A wide variety of drama and/or writing activities can be developed at the end of the story. These could include setting up a public railway inquiry about the incidents, which could include interviewing witnesses and preparing witness statements and newspaper reports.

'The Call'

Improvisations
- After the first phone call.
- The scene when they are back home at the end of it all
- Harry's phone calls in the past.

'He never thought that telephones got past locked doors'
Drama or writing activities can be developed, not directly connected to the story, that fit/explain this idea.

Continuing the story
Stop reading the story at:

... And like a sleepwalker Meg turned to follow ...

Ask the pupils to continue the story and/or create still pictures of the scene.

TEACHING AND LEARNING COMMENTARY

For one or more of these scenes, pupils can be asked (in role) to speak their thoughts or be questioned in role to develop their ideas and establish why they have chosen the particular sentences. This is a good way of encouraging pupils to acquire the habit of looking for evidence in the text and, as a result, using quotations effectively in their writing

Numerous opportunities exist for writing activities. Links can also be made with media (storyboards, analysis of the film version) and the work could be developed in to the Media assignment for GCSE English.

The aim is to follow a similar approach to each story. Read parts of the story at a time. This allows for further links between the stories to be developed. Pupils often pick an aspect for comparison just by undertaking the similar activities.

During these activities, the pupils begin, through the use of role, to consider the characters. They can again be questioned in role or speak their thoughts to develop this understanding.

This can be approached through further drama work, discussion or writing tasks. The need for prediction encourages pupils to analyse the text, searching for clues within the story.

For one or more of these scenes, pupils can be asked (in role) to speak their thoughts or be questioned in role to develop their ideas and establish why they have chosen the particular sentences. This is a good way of encouraging pupils to acquire the habit of looking for evidence in the text and, as a result, using quotations effectively in their writing

NC/NLS REFERENCES

ACTIVITIES AND APPROACHES

TEACHING AND LEARNING COMMENTARY

EN1   Drama: 4a

Significant sentences and scenes
As with 'The Signalman', ask groups of pupils to choose significant sentences from the whole story and present them in a tableau effect.

EN2   Understanding texts:
1a,b,c,g,h

Layers
(See 'Layers of wallpaper' on page 93.) Use wallpaper (or pupils in layers) as a way of analysing the story and the different layers that exist within it: the narrator controlling the layers, building them up, visual images existing on different layers, the power of imagination to create and believe that different layers exist, etc.

'A Basket Full of Wallpaper'

EN1   Drama: 4a,
Drama activities: 11a

Working in role
- Conversations that show the rumours circulating about Osobe
- The scene at the table, discussing the lack of work, need for money, etc.
- Beach stones / paper dolls / wallpaper – drama. Creating symbolism
- First day at work – conversations about it
- The invented stories/rumours
- The epilogue – life now
- The funeral.

The aim is to follow a similar approach to each story. Read parts of the story at a time. This allows for further links between the stories to be developed. Pupils often pick an aspect for comparison just by undertaking the similar activities.

As with 'The Signalman', requiring pupils to create pictures that can be given sentences from another part of the story, leads to close reading of the text and a focus on language, imagery and authorial purpose.

EN1   Drama: 4a,
Drama activities: 11 a

Still pictures/use of visual images
Create still pictures that depict the wallpapering at different stages in the story. Ask the pupils whether they present a neutral image or not.

Encourage pupils to create visual links with different parts of the story (see '"The Signalman": the beginning and the end' on page 95.)

EN1   Drama: 4a
EN2   Understanding texts: 1a,d,g,k

Significant sentences and scenes
As with 'The Signalman', ask groups of pupils to choose significant sentences from the whole story and present them in a tableau effect.

EN2   Understanding texts:
1a,b,c,d,g,h,k

Layers
(See 'Layers of wallpaper' on page 93.) Use wallpaper (or pupils in layers) as a way of analysing the story and the different layers that exist within it: the narrator controlling the layers, visual images, power of imagination to create and believe that different layers exist, etc. Did Osobe have different layers to his character, or not?

The idea of layers is a useful way of exploring both text and drama. By requiring the pupils to actually represent these layers by standing in lines and moving according to the discussions that take place, they are encouraged to question and understand the relationships that exist between writer, reader and text.

Linked ideas
Work could be developed by exploring the following in more detail:
- Hiroshima
- The power of imagination in stories and the media
- The role if the narrator in fiction and the media.

A number of other activities can be developed by exploring these issues and events.

GCSE assignment

Once a number of the drama activities have been completed, students will have a detailed understanding of the texts and be able to make links between them. The use of drama means that these links are not just thematic but recognise the authorial styles and techniques used. The students will feel confident in handling the texts and be able to find quotations easily. With very little preparation they will be able to write on one of the essay questions provided below.

Links and layers: essay titles

You have been studying the following short stories:

'The Signal Man'

'The Call'

'A Basket Full of Wallpaper'

You need to choose *one* essay question from the selection below.

You *must* refer to 'The Signal Man' in your answer *and one of the other stories* (either 'The Call' or 'A Basket Full of Wallpaper').

Remember to use quotations throughout to support your comments and check your work very carefully when you have finished to make sure you have not made any spelling or punctuation mistakes.

1 Compare and contrast the ways in which the reader, structure and ideas are controlled by the authors' use of the narrator/narrative voice.

2 For what purposes and to what effect do the authors use and develop the relationship between narrator and central character.

3 The reader takes an active role in the stories we have studied. Discuss how the way the stories are written develops the reader's involvement and the themes, ideas and characters that are presented.

4 The jobs that the characters have all influence the content, themes, structure and style of the stories. Compare the ways that the authors develop the 'role' of two of the following: the Samaritan, the wallpaperer, the signalman.

5 How do the different authors explore the use of suspense and the power of the imagination in both the narrative events and the reader's mind.

Links and layers: essay titles

You have been studying the following short stories:

'The Signal Man'

'The Call'

'A Basket Full of Wallpaper'

You need to choose *one* essay question from the selection below.

You *must* refer to 'The Signal Man' in your answer *and one of the other stories* (either 'The Call' or 'A Basket Full of Wallpaper').

Remember to use quotations throughout to support your comments and check your work very carefully when you have finished to make sure you have not made any spelling or punctuation mistakes.

1 Compare and contrast the ways in which the reader, structure and ideas are controlled by the authors' use of the narrator/narrative voice.

2 For what purposes and to what effect do the authors use and develop the relationship between narrator and central character.

3 The reader takes an active role in the stories we have studied. Discuss how the way the stories are written develops the reader's involvement and the themes, ideas and characters that are presented.

4 The jobs that the characters have all influence the content, themes, structure and style of the stories. Compare the ways that the authors develop the 'role' of two of the following: the Samaritan, the wallpaperer, the signalman.

5 How do the different authors explore the use of suspense and the power of the imagination in both the narrative events and the reader's mind.

Unit 15
Shakespeare and drama: exploring the social and historical values

Shakespeare's *Macbeth* describes a feudal warrior society from the perspective of early modern London. The qualities that were valued in such a society – total loyalty to the feudal lord, the ability to kill ruthlessly – were no longer widely shared in Shakespeare's day, when the rule of law, social mobility and personal ambition were much more valued in Jacobean London. *Macbeth* has been seen by some critics as a man trapped in the contradictions of feudal ideology, or perhaps as living as a modern individualist in a feudal world. See Graham Holderness (1989) '"Shakespeare's Tragic Heroes Are Fatally Flawed." Discuss', *Critical Survey*, 1, 1 and Jonathan Dollimore (1993) *Radical Tragedy*, Harvester, Hemel Hempstead (second edition).

Resources

A copy of the text (references given are to the *Cambridge School Shakespeare*, ed. Rex Gibson, CUP, 1993)

Pictures of imperial statuary, if available

Whiteboard/sugar paper

Drama studio or classroom

Learning objectives

Through a variety of drama activities, pupils are encouraged to reflect on the values of the feudal society depicted in the play and become more comfortable with speaking the play's language.

Extracts from the units ...

Talk about (or show, if you have suitable illustrations) statuary groups that show heroes surrounded by the symbols of their conquests. There are often allegorical figures representing qualities, as well as other people, in these groups. Set half the class to produce a statue that shows either Macdonwald or Macbeth, drawing on the language of the text as much as possible for the details of the statue. Macbeth is to be celebrated by the statue, Macdonwald condemned. Alternatively, show both men in a single statuary group.

Commentary:
Close focus on textual detail here. Pupil collaboration is vital.

Macbeth can be shown at one or more or three points in the battle. Encourage the work to show exactly what the language says as visually as possible.

(All references are to the programmes of study at KS 3/4.)

NC REFERENCES	ACTIVITIES AND APPROACHES	TEACHING AND LEARNING COMMENTARY

EN1   Group discussion and interaction: 3a,e

Drama : 4a

Language variation: 6f

EN2   Understanding texts: 1a, c

EN1   Speaking: 1a

Listening: 2a, b, f.

Group discussion and interaction: 3a,b,de

Drama: 4a

ACTIVITIES AND APPROACHES

Tuning the pupils into the language

Start with the pupils sitting in a circle with l.2. 7–24 in front of them. Explain that you're going to be looking at the kind of society in which the play is set. This will require some work off the text to look at the values we expect of society today. First, however, they're going to play with the language of the text a little.

Ask them if they can recall who the sergeant is, and what he is describing to whom at this early point in the play. Read this section around the class a few times, changing the speaker each time there is a punctuation mark (full stop, dash, comma in this case). Don't stop to discuss meaning at this point. They'll soon become familiar with what their line(s) might be, and know whom they follow in the order of speaking. When they're used to getting through the speech in this way, push back the chairs and do the speech standing up; then walking round the room, weaving in and out of one another. Get them to do it sitting on the floor around the edge of the room, stage whispering it; get them to shout it aloud; get them to do it with an accompanying gesture for their part. Back in the circle again, discuss the meaning of the whole speech in a group, making sure it is grasped as fully as possible – they will be very familiar with the text after ten or twelve readings aloud, after all.

Heroic statues and modern values

Talk about (or show, if you have suitable illustrations) statuary groups that show heroes surrounded by the symbols of their conquests. There are often allegorical figures representing qualities, as well as other people, in these groups. Set half the class to produce a statue that shows either Macdonwald or Macbeth, drawing on the language of the text as much as possible for the details of the statue. Macbeth is to be *celebrated* by the statue, Macdonwald *condemned*. Alternatively, show both men in a single statuary group.

It may help to write on the board the particular qualities or pieces of action the pupils have identified and you wish each group to illustrate.

Alternatively, show as a sequence of moving symbolic images: the Macbeth group's action can have three distinct phases.

The other half of the class are given a totally different task. They are to be form tutors of Year 11 in a secondary school. The head teacher is about to give a final assembly to the year before they start their GCSEs and leave the school. In it, he/she wants to tell them how he/she thinks they should live their lives in society today in order to make Britain a good place to live – he/she is that kind

TEACHING AND LEARNING COMMENTARY

All the pupils need to feel involved in both language and process. If they are only guessing what the language means in their own terms a main teaching point – that Shakespeare is showing that the values of feudal society are not the values of early modern, let alone modern, Britain – will be lost. This process should involve them all in the action, and encourage them to understand the text clearly.

Get them (or you!) to be explicit about metaphors like 'swarm' (line 12) and the goddess Fortune being 'a rebel's whore'.

Discussion here of the impact and effect of figurative language.

Close focus on textual detail here. Pupil collaboration is vital.

Macbeth can be shown at one or more of three points in the battle. Encourage the work to show exactly what the language says as visually as possible.

Reflection on moral and civic values. Speaking and listening skills of arguing and explaining.

ACTIVITIES AND APPROACHES

TEACHING AND LEARNING COMMENTARY

of head. The Year 11 tutors have been asked to draw up a list of values they think should be referred to in the speech. What would they include? Tolerance of others? Standing up for what you believe in? Loyalty to the government? Non-violence? Start to make a list on a flip chart/board. They must hurry, however. List the ones they can all quickly agree on.

If the word 'values' poses a problem for the pupils ask them for a set of 'golden rules' that, if followed by all, would make the world a better place. Try to avoid listing specific crimes or acts. The aim is to create a modern context for criticism that sees the play historically and politically, rather in terms of character or a historical sense of 'good' and 'evil'.

When the statue groups are ready, return (in role as the head) to the Year 11 tutors. You have heard there's a new exhibition of statues showing life in Macbeth's day at a gallery. You want the tutors to see these because it may help them in their task. They should bring their copies of *Macbeth*. Moving briefly out of role, ask the statue groups, one after another, to freeze after a count of five. Back in role, examine the statues and discuss with the 'tutors' what the statues depict. What quality or qualities do the statues show that they might want to include in their list? What qualities would they want to miss out, or even actively discourage?

It is important to praise the work and to find the textual details that can relate to key feudal values: skill at violence and unconditional loyalty as central virtues in the play. They may find other ideas too. Critical discussion of these values in a modern context may take place here.

Modern values and feudal values

Back in a circle again, some discussion can take place about what it is that Duncan values in a man, and what a modern head teacher might value. Written work might consolidate what these values might be at this point. It might take the form of a close reading of the language of the text, followed by a comment on the values presented from a modern perspective.

This is the point where a historical perspective about value systems should begin to develop.

Representing textual images

Now work on l.7.1–28. Do a warm-up first, however. Brainstorm a few proverbs on the board and then ask groups of three or four pupils to act them out as visually as possible: 'Look before you leap'; 'A stitch in time saves nine'; 'Pride comes before a fall'. Watch these. Then return to the text.

This is a difficult soliloquy. Read around the group a few times as before, with a bit of teacher glossing at times. Then ask the same groups of three or four to show visually, with words if they like, the images from the text listed below. They can make up their own context and add their own language to the work if doing so will help.

we but teach
Bloody instructions, which being taught, return
To plague th'inventor (8–10)

This even-handed justice
Commends th'ingredience of our poisoned chalice
To our own lips. (10–12)

NC/NLS REFERENCES

ACTIVITIES AND APPROACHES

TEACHING AND LEARNING COMMENTARY

First, as I am his kinsman and his subject,
Strong both against the deed; then, as his host,
Who should against his murderer shut the door,
Not bear the knife myself. (13–16)

Watch these, or some of them.

Killing a man then

Now organise the pupils in threes. Two will speak the speech, changing speaker each time there is a punctuation mark. They sit facing one another. It is visiting time at the prison, and they are having a conversation which the third, the patrolling warder, mustn't overhear. Quietly and tensely they speak the speech, as urgently and meaningfully as possible. Whenever the patrolling warder gets near they stop talking and try not to look suspicious.

Now read around the group l.7.29–58. Ask pairs to read the extract to each other a couple of times, one playing Macbeth and the other his wife. Ask pairs to discuss the reasons Lady Macbeth uses to persuade her husband that he should kill King Duncan.

Killing a man now

The same pairs improvise a modern version where one person uses the same arguments to persuade one man to kill another so that they can achieve their ambition. In the modern version the 'Macbeth' is allowed to argue back, and to use the arguments a modern person might use. Freeze the action and see a minute or so of argument. Then carry on again. Freeze and see another couple.

Concluding activity

Split the class in half. One half must choose a quotation either from Macbeth, giving a reason why he doesn't want to kill the king, or Lady Macbeth, giving a reason why he should. The other half of the class should devise a phrase in their own words expressing an opinion on the murder one way or the other. One pupil, as Macbeth, now has to walk down an alley with pro-murder people whispering at him on one side and anti-murder whisperers on the other. 'Macbeth' has to stop and react to each as they go by. Make it as powerful a performance as you can.

Back in the group circle again, try to summarise the values of the society in which Macbeth lives. How are they different from ours? To what extent do they contradict each other? If killing the most powerful potential opponent makes you a true man, how can that be reconciled with unconditional loyalty to your superior? How can meekness and bloodthirstiness sit side by side as admirable qualities in this world? How can Macbeth live by all of them? Are

---

This work is at a tangent to the main objective, but will both increase the pupils' sense of the speech's dramatic tension and make them still more familiar with the rhythms and movements of the verse.

Close textual engagement.
It is not necessary to *perform* these unless you want to. Understanding is more important here than acting.

Effective improvisation. Skills of argument and persuasion. Pupils will need a specific context to do this well, so you should be prepared to provide a couple. This is a point where the historical contrast should emerge strongly again.

The ability to collaborate in a performance.
This work should function as a fitting dramatic conclusion to the unit as a whole. You may want to rehearse it a couple of times before a final 'performance'.

Reflection on values; on historical difference and historical relativism.

EN1 Drama: 4a,b,c
EN2 Understanding texts: 1c,d,h

EN1 Speaking: 1c
     Listening: 2b,2c,e
     Drama: 4a

EN1 Drama: 4a, b

EN1 Group discussion and
     interaction: 3a,b,c
EN2 Understanding texts: 1b,c,d,h

ACTIVITIES AND APPROACHES

the Macbeths actually more 'modern' in their behaviour and values than mediaeval? Does it make any sense to talk about Macbeth as 'good' or 'evil' in a modern sense?

Follow-up work

Parts of this scheme could be adapted, with a commentary written by the pupils, for a presentation to other pupils studying the play about the feudal values of the play and how Macbeth tries to live by them.

Coursework units could focus on the reasons given by Macbeth and Lady Macbeth for and against killing the king in I.7, and the language used; or, broadly, on what the play's values are and how they explain Macbeth's behaviour.

Assessment

Discussions and presentations could be assessed for Speaking and Listening. Final written work, as stated, could be submitted as coursework

Glossary

Dramatic conventions used in this publication

Action narration: a stylised convention which requires each participant to pause and verbalise motives and descriptions of actions before they undertake them in an improvisation

Communal voice: the group operates as commentator on the action while speaking from the same perspective, or individuals speak the words of one of the characters in the drama

Communal writing: similar to 'communal voice', but the contributions from the group are written down to be considered at a later date

Conscience alley: a group divided into two lines faces each other. A pupil (or teacher) in role as a character in the drama walks between the two lines as individuals speak out what is in the character's conscience. This may be set up so that one line represents the positive aspects of the character's dilemma nd the other line, the negative

Flashback: replay of important sections to allow for group scrutiny. Can be done in real time, slow-motion or as a series of tableaux

Forum theatre: action by an individual or small group enacted in front of the whole group. Ownership of the action is shared by all, thereby encouraging intervention, pausing, suggestion, replay and commentary

Freeze-frame – marking the moment – tableau: small group 'freezing' of a significant moment to allow for group observation and analysis

Guided tour: in pairs, A (with eyes open) leads B (with eyes closed) slowly through an imaginary environment, providing a spoken commentary. The environment or location may be based on text but will usually be stimulated by a printed or projected pictorial map. Roles can be reversed to enable parity of experience

Hot-seating: placing one person in role under scrutiny– usually done by seating the individual and directing questions at her/him from the group

Improvised drama: encouraging participants to openly explore an issue or situation through the perspective of their adopted roles

Mantle of the expert: an individual or group of characters are imbued with specialist knowledge about a subject. This allows them to speak with 'authority' to the rest of the group

Mime: movement without words depicting and often replaying a significant moment

Ritual: a stylised enactment of moments of high social and cultural significance, e.g. initiation into a gang

Role on the wall: a useful 'communal' method of building a role as a group – ideas are collected from the group and progressively displayed – usually done with sugar paper and 'Post-It' notes as a 'work in progress' document

Role reversal: a technique of encouraging participants to swap roles so that different perspectives can be experienced and considered from within the drama

Scripted drama: using written text to shape the structure of the piece

Sculpting: participants offer suggestions to place an individual in a significant, frozen position so that considered analysis can be made

Small group playmaking: small groups of participants plan and present pieces of drama that explore the issues and context of the work

Teacher in role: a crucial technique whereby the group leader adopts a role (which could be central to the drama) that offers a model of appropriate language and behaviour. Sometimes the teacher will deliberately choose a low status role to offer an alternative perspective

Thought-tracking: giving those in role the opportunity to voice their inner thoughts and feelings by stopping the action and making the distinction between their inner and outer utterances explicit

Warm-ups: structured playful activities designed to forge a dynamic within the group. Often contains a 'serious' link with the work to follow

Writing in role: a technique whereby participants write from the point of view of one of the roles. This enables different perspectives and viewpoints to be explored in greater depth

Bibliography

Ackroyd, J. (2000) *Literacy Alive*. Hodder & Stoughton. ISBN 0340 75774 4

Baldwin, P. (1971) *Stimulating Drama (Primary)*. National Drama. ISBN 1 83750 500 0

Baldwin, P. and Hendy, L. (1996) *The Drama Book (Primary)*. HarperCollins. ISBN 0 00316 146 3

Bolton, G. (1979) *Towards a Theory of Drama in Education*. Longman. ISBN 0582 36189 9

Bolton, G. (1984) *Drama as Education*. Longman. ISBN 0 582 36198 2

Bolton, G. (1991) *New Perspectives on Classroom Drama*. Simon & Schuster. ISBN 0 75010195 4

Fleming, M. (1995) *Starting Drama Teaching*. David Fulton Publishers. ISBN 1 85346 297 7

Gibson, R. (1998) *Teaching Shakespeare*. Cambridge University Press. ISBN 0 52157 788 8

Grainger, T. and Cremin, M. (2000) *Resourcing Classroom Drama 5–8*. NATE. ISBN 0 901291 78 1

Grainger, T. and Cremin, M. (2000) *Resourcing Classroom Drama 8–14*. NATE. ISBN 0 901291 79 X

Harrison, L.S. (1998) *Dance and Drama*. Scholastic. ISBN 0590 53791 1

Harrison, L.S. (1999) *Curriculum Bank: Key Stage One Drama*. Scholastic. ISBN 0 590 53784 9

Harrison, L.S. (1999) *Curriculum Bank: Key Stage Two Drama*. Scholastic. ISBN 0 590 53785 7

Lamden, G. (2000) *Devising*. Hodder & Stoughton. ISBN 0 340 78008 8

Linnel, R. (1982) *Approaching Classroom Drama*. Edward Arnold. ISBN 0 71310 724 3

NATE 9–14 Committee (1993) *Move Back the Desks*. NATE. ISBN 0 90129 129 3

Neelands, J. (1983) *Making Sense of Drama*. Heinemann. ISBN 0 43518 658 2

Neelands, J. (1992) *Learning through Imagined Experience*. Hodder & Stoughton. ISBN 0 3405 4258 6

Neelands, J. (1998) *Beginning Drama 11–14*. David Fulton Publishers. ISBN 1 85346 528 3

Neelands, J. (2000) *Structuring Drama Work*. Cambridge University Press. ISBN 0 52178 729 7

Nixon, J. (1987) *Teaching Drama*. Macmillan Education. ISBN 0 33342 000 4

O'Neill, C. and Lambert, A. (1984) *Drama Structures*. Hutchinson. ISBN 0 74870 191 5

O'Neill, C., Lambert, A., Linnet, R. and Warr-Wood, J. (1976) *Drama Guidelines*. Heinemann. ISBN 0 43518 670 1

Owens, A. and Barber, K. (1997) *Dramaworks*. Carel Press. ISBN 1 87236 532 9

Rainer, J. and Bunyan, P. (1996) *The Patchwork Quilt*. NATE. ISBN 0 901291 46 3

Readman, G. & Lamont, G. (1994) *Drama Handbook for Primary Teachers*. BBC Educational Publishing. ISBN 0 563 35525 5

Reynolds, P. (1991) *Practical Approaches to Teaching Shakespeare*. Oxford University Press. ISBN 0 19831095401

Rooke, C. (1998) *Drama: Policy and Practice in the Primary School*. Available from: London Drama Book Service (Tel. 0207 7224730)

Taylor, K. (ed.) (1991) *Drama Strategies*. Heinemann. ISBN 0 43518 671 X

Winston, J. (2000) *Drama Literacy and Moral Education 5–11*. David Fulton Publishers. ISBN 1 85346 636 0

Winston, J. and Tandy M. (1998) *Beginning Drama 4–11*. David Fulton Publishers. ISBN 1 85346 527 5